A Simp

Outlook 98

M. Cassade

Prentice Hall

London New York Toronto Sydney Tokyo Singapore Madrid
Mexico City Munich Paris

First published in 1998 as Outlook 98 – Se Former en 1 Jour by
Simon & Schuster Macmillan (France)
This edition published 1999 by
Prentice Hall
An imprint of
Pearson Education Limited
Edinburgh Gate
Harlow
Essex CM20 2JE, England

Translated by Berlitz Translation Services UK, Baldock, Hertfordshire

Printed and bound in Great Britain by
Redwood Books, Trowbridge, Wiltshire

Library of Congress Cataloging-in-Publication Data

Available from the publisher

British Library Cataloguing in Publication Data

A catalogue record for this book is available from the British Library
ISBN 0-13-021257-1

12345 03 02 01 00 99

Table of Contents

Introduction

As you will discover in this book, Outlook 98 is perfect for managing and organising your life: it is a comprehensive e-mail client (MS-Mail, Internet, X400, CompuServe, MSN, etc.), a message sorter, a personal and group scheduler, a contact and address database, a desk diary, a mini project manager and a tool for monitoring your work – all in one. Outlook helps you with all the tasks you have to perform.

Who is this book intended for?

This book is intended for all those who are already familiar with Outlook 97 and who want to quickly acquaint themselves with Outlook 98. Beginners will find all they need to start using the program without difficulty, along with advice on how to make best use of it. More experienced users will be able to increase their knowledge of Outlook 98 and take advantage of all the new facilities and time-saving features available in this version.

Organisation of the book

The first two hours of this book are intended for beginners in particular. Here they will discover the various components of Outlook and their functions. The principle behind Outlook is the display of information. At the end of each hour, a table will list all the keyboard shortcuts learned in that hour, and a second table will summarise the symbols learned in the hour. These will allow you to quickly locate different types of information.

- **Hour 1** gives an overview of navigating through the application and tips for making rapid progress.
- **Hour 2** introduces the various components of Outlook: the Outlook bar, the suggested groups, the different folders and the help they contain.
- **Hour 3** gets to the heart of the matter. You will start by discovering the Contacts folder and how to manage it, then you will learn how to import information and look at the Address Book.
- **Hour 4** explains how to use e-mail, and starts with receiving and handling messages.
- **Hour 5** deals with sending messages. You will look at handling and creating messages, the folders in which you can keep them, etc.
- **Hour 6** shows you how to use the Outlook scheduler known as the Calendar folder. Here you will discover how to plan your appointments and meetings, and how to keep a list of tasks to be carried out.
- **Hour 7** looks at the Tasks folder: this will help you to plan, monitor and quantify the various tasks for which you are responsible in the course of your work.
- **Hour 8** will show you the Journal and Notes folders, which correspond respectively to a log of your activities and to the electronic equivalent of 'post-it' notes.
- **Hour 9** shows you how to organise meetings and tasks taking into account the commitments of your colleagues.
- **Hour 10** explains how to print, how to define a page layout, and how to import files from another program into Outlook.
- **Hour 11** teaches you how to use the examples provided, how to search for information, how to organise it, and how to create links between information items.
- **Hour 12** shows you how to "surf" the Internet using Outlook.

SPECIAL ICONS

In this book you will find boxes highlighting special points.

These notes provide additional information on the subject concerned.

These notes indicate a variety of shortcuts: keyboard shortcuts, 'Wizard' options, techniques reserved for experts, etc.

These notes warn you of any risks associated with a particular action and, where necessary, show you how to avoid any pitfalls.

Hour 1

Discovery and navigation

The contents for this hour

- Introducing Outlook
- Installation of Outlook
- Discovering Outlook
- Navigating in Outlook
- Executing commands

Introducing Outlook

Outlook is an office information manager which helps you to:

- exchange and share information using e-mail;
- plan your day;

- share information with other Office programs (Word, Excel, PowerPoint, etc.);
- manage information, including e-mail messages, contacts, appointments, meetings, tasks, etc.; and
- connect to the Web.

Basic components

In your office, you use a diary, an address book, drawers, filing cabinets, and so on, to organise your work. Each day you receive mail, take messages and update your diary. Outlook recreates the organisation of your office in the form of folders: these are the Outlook folders. All these folders are incorporated in the Outlook bar. You simply click to open a "filing cabinet", consult a folder, find an address or call a customer.

Here is a list of the Outlook folders and their functions:

- **Outlook Today.** This displays all the useful information for the day and allows you to initialise Outlook according to your day's work.
- **Inbox.** This allows you to send and receive e-mail messages, to view them before opening them, and to follow up and monitor your mail.
- **Calendar.** This is your diary. It allows you to monitor your activities and plan your appointments, meetings, special events, etc. Its date navigator gives direct access to information concerning your use of time, and monitors tasks to be performed.
- **Contacts.** This is your address book, and it allows you to update and monitor information concerning your professional or private contacts. You can sort it, group it into categories or even link files to it.
- **Tasks.** This is the schedule for your different tasks, and it allows you to organise, prioritise and monitor the progress of all your tasks. You can also allocate tasks to your colleagues and receive progress reports from them.

- **Journal.** This is your "daily log". This allows you to record interactions with your contacts, to store data, messages and important files.
- **Notes.** This corresponds to electronic "post-it" notes. This folder allows you to make notes, send them to a colleague, etc. So, whenever you have an idea, you can "scribble" it in this folder and recall it when you need to.
- **Recycle bin.** This is your "wastepaper basket". Anything you delete is put in this folder. As long as you don't empty it, the information remains available.

Installation of Outlook

The Setup Wizard is an efficient guide which will help you through this process, automatically detecting existing installations (e.g. Exchange Server, Address Book, profiles in use or others) and seeing that they are incorporated into the new version.

System and hardware configuration

To install Outlook 98, you must have a Pentium PC, Windows 95 or NT, 16 MB of RAM (32 MB preferably), 100 MB of free disk space and a pointing device (mouse, IntelliPoint, etc.). If you want to connect to the Web, you must also have a modem.

Installation procedures

To install Outlook 98, you must carry out the following procedures:

1. Insert the Outlook 98 CD-ROM in the drive.
2. Click on **Start**, then choose **Settings**.
3. From the cascade menu, click on **Control Panel.**
4. Double click on **Add/Remove Programs**.
5. In the Add/Remove Programs Properties dialog box, click (if required) on the **Install/Uninstall** tab.

6. Click on **Install**.

   The Install Program from Floppy Disk or CD-ROM dialog box appears.

7. Click on **Next**.

   The Run Installation Program dialog box appears. (see Figure 1.1).

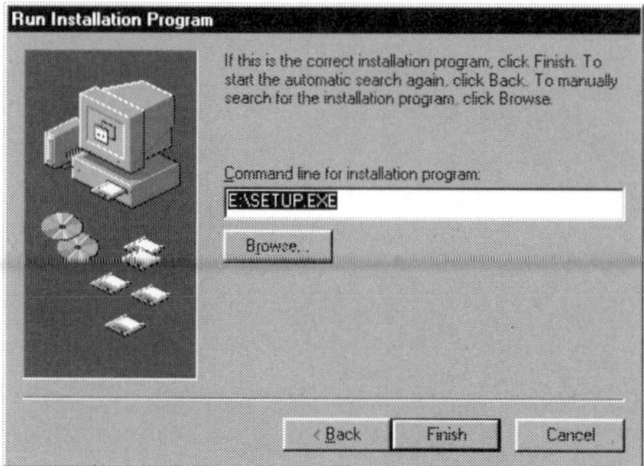

Figure 1.1: The Run Installation Program dialog box shows the access path to your CD-ROM

8. Click on **Finish**.

   The first Outlook 98 installation dialog box is displayed.

9. Click on **Next**.

10. Enter your name in the **user name** field.

11. Enter the name of your company (or other organisation) in the **Organisation** field.

12. Click on **Next**.

    You must choose the type of installation required. By default, **standard** installation is suggested. The types of installation are:

    - **Standard.** Installs Outlook, Internet Explorer 4.0 and Outlook help files.
    - **Minimal.** Installs Outlook and Internet Explorer 4.0.

   - **Extended.** Installs Outlook, Internet Explorer 4.0, Outlook help, a choice of Office Assistant, the PIM (Personal Information Manager) converters and system tools.
   - **Complete.** Installs the same applications as the **Extended** installation, but adds development tools and additional components of Outlook.

13. After choosing the type of installation required, click on **Next**.
14. Two options are offered. If you have Outlook 97 already installed and it is this application which currently manages your e-mail, click on **Yes**, then on **Next**. If you have not installed Outlook 97 or Outlook 97 does not manage your e-mail, click on **No**, then on **Next**. Now select the e-mail program from the displayed list, then click on **Next**.
15. Whether you chose **Yes** or **No**, you come to the dialog box which displays the Outlook installation folder. If you want to change this folder, click on **Browse**, then choose the required folder.
16. Click on **Next**.
17. After a few seconds, Windows prepares the installation. Click on **Next** to begin the installation.

    Windows performs the installation, which will take some time.
18. When installation is complete, click on **OK**.

    The computer will automatically reboot (reset) itself.

    After rebooting, Internet Explorer 4.0, the Internet tools, security and the Desktop parameters will have been installed.

Close the Control Panel.

Once installation is complete, three icons are displayed on the Windows Desktop. By double-clicking on any of them you will be able to run Internet Explorer 4.0, Outlook or Outlook Express.

Discovering Outlook

First of all, we will start Outlook, get to know its main screen, and learn how to use its various tools.

Starting Outlook

Outlook is started from Windows Desktop. To do this, double click on the Outlook shortcut (see Figure 1.2).

Figure 1.2: The Outlook shortcut icon

Screen

The screen displays different components allowing you to navigate within the program and to activate commands (see Figure 1.3).

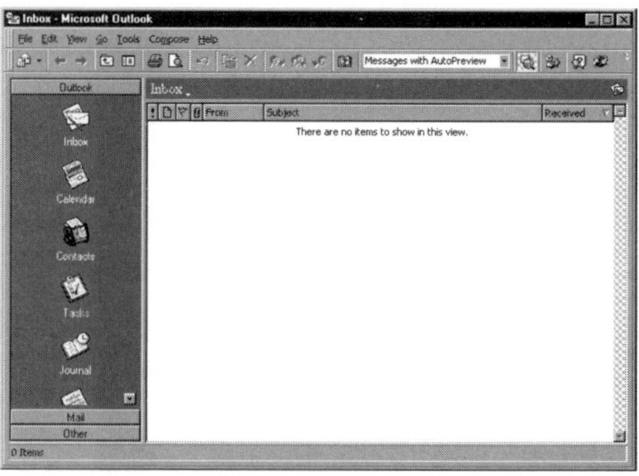

Figure 1.3: The Outlook screen displays the Inbox folder by default

Click on **Close** in the Office Assistant button.

It is possible that one or more of the items displayed in Figure 1.3 will not appear.

To display a missing item:

1. Click on the **View** menu; a tick will appear next to the active items.
2. Click on the non-active commands for the missing items such as **Toolbars**, **Status Bars** or **Outlook Bars**.

System buttons

The system buttons are located at the extreme right of the title bar. They allow you to close, enlarge, restore or reduce the window. They are common to all software which runs under Windows 95. See Table 1.1 to see how to use them.

Table 1.1: Using the system buttons.

Button	Description
	Enlarges the window to its maximum size
	Reduces the window to a button in the Taskbar
	When you are in full screen mode, reduces the window to half its size
	Closes Outlook

Context-sensitive menus and right-clicking

The actions which you can apply to different items displayed on screen are grouped together in a context-sensitive menu. The term "context-sensitive" means that the content of the menu varies according to the object from which you activated the menu. Throughout this book, we will concentrate on illustrating procedures which use the various context-sensitive menus. You display a context-sensitive menu by clicking the right mouse button (see Figure 1.4).

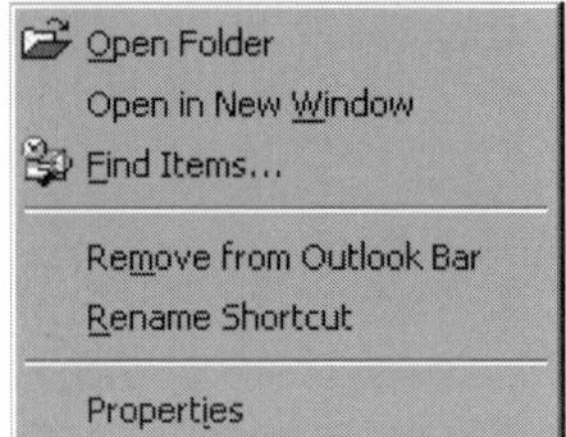

Figure 1.4: Context-sensitive menu of the Inbox folder

Navigating in Outlook

Now you will learn how to navigate within the various components of Outlook.

Toolbars

By default, Outlook displays a Standard toolbar (see Figure 1.5) which allows you to speed up your work as it contains buttons for carrying out the most common actions. To access a command, simply click on the relevant button. The Standard toolbar varies according to the folder in use.

Outlook has two other toolbars: Remote and Advanced. To display another toolbar, right-click in the Standard toolbar, then select the desired toolbar in the context-sensitive menu which is then displayed. You can also click on **View, Toolbars.** From the cascading menu, select the toolbar you want.

Figure 1.5: The Standard toolbar of the Inbox folder

Customising a toolbar

You can easily add buttons to a toolbar for the commands you use often and which do not appear in the Standard toolbar.

To customise a toolbar, right-click in the Standard toolbar. Select **Customise**, then click on the **Commands** tab (see Figure 1.6). In the Categories section, select the menu containing the command to be added to the toolbar. The suggested buttons are displayed in the Commands section. Click on the button to be added then, holding down the mouse button, drag the mouse cursor to the Standard toolbar and release the button. Click on **Close** in the Customise dialog box.

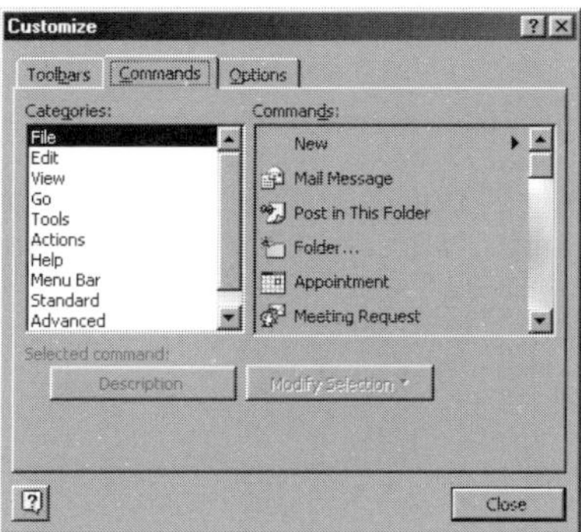

Figure 1.6: Customising your toolbars

*To delete a button from a toolbar, right-click in the toolbar, then select **Customise**. In the toolbar, click on the button to delete, then drag it outside the bar and release the mouse button. Click on **Close**.*

Taskbar

This is located at the bottom of the screen. In addition to the Start button, it displays buttons representing all the active tasks.

Menu bar

This is located below the title bar. In this bar, Outlook offers pop-up menus which group together the different commands for the application.

To open a menu, click on the desired menu or press Alt together with the letter underlined in the menu bar: for example, press **Alt-F** to open the File menu.

Selection of commands

In a drop-down menu, a list of commands is offered. When the mouse cursor touches a command, it is highlighted to show it has been selected for activation. To choose a command in a menu, click on the desired command or enter the letter corresponding to the underlined letter in the command to be activated (this is a shortcut).

The menus contain a number of indicators corresponding to a keyboard shortcut, a sub-menu or a dialog box. See Table 1.2 for a description of each of the indicators.

Table 1.2: The different command indicators.

Indicator	Description
Command in black	Offers a directly accessible command
Command “greyed”	Means that this command is currently unavailable
Command followed by an arrow	Offers a sub-menu for this command
Command followed by three dots	Opens a dialog box

Table 1.2: The different command indicators (cont.).

Indicator	Description
Command preceded by a tick	Indicates that the command is active. Clicking on it deactivates it (the tick disappears)
Command preceded by a black circle	Indicates that it is a group of commands and that the command is active
Key shortcut	Indicates the letter you must enter to activate a command using the keyboard
Keyboard shortcut	Indicates the keys you must press to activate this command without opening the menu

To close a menu without selecting a command, simply click outside the drop-down menu or press ***Escape*** *twice.*

Dialog boxes

When you select a command followed by three dots, a dialog box is displayed. This allows you to interact with Outlook by telling it the choice you want to make from the range of options offered.

Let's open the Options dialog box, from which you can make your choices for customising Outlook.

To open the Options dialog box:

1. Click on **Tools**, then select **Options**.
2. Click on the **Preferences** tab (see Figure 1.7).

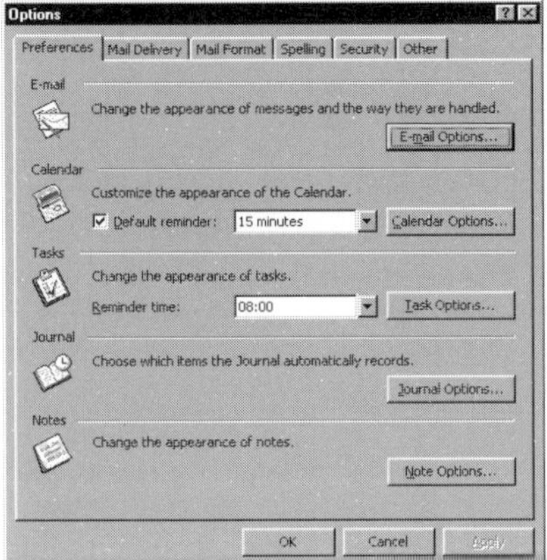

Figure 1.7: The dialog box for the Options command in the Tools menu

A number of items appear in the dialog box: see Table 1.3 for how to use each of these items.

Table 1.3: The components of dialog boxes.

Component	Description
Tabs	Located at the top of a dialogue window, tabs group together options of a similar type. Click on the tab to display its page.
Option boxes	Preceded by a circle. You can select only one at a time. Simply click on one of them to activate it. When it is active, a black circle appears inside the box.
Tick boxes	Preceded by a square. You can select any number at once. Simply click on one of them to activate it. When it is active, a black tick appears inside the box.

Table 1.3: The components of dialog boxes (cont).

Component	Description
Pop-up lists	Click on the arrow to the right of the list to pop it up, then choose the required item.
Text fields	Intended for any text you have to enter. To change text, select the content of the field, then enter the new text.

3. After making your choices by means of the items in Table 1.3, click on **OK** to confirm them. Table 1.4 shows the different options for closing a dialog box.

Table 1.4: The command buttons for closing a dialog box.

Button	Description
OK	Confirms the choices you have made. You can also press **Enter**.
APPLY	Applies the selections made in the dialog box.
CANCEL	Ignores the modifications made in the dialog box. You can also press **Escape**.
SAVE	Saves the selections.
END	Confirms the choices you have made.
BROWSE	Displays another dialog box to perform searches.
OPEN	Displays another dialog box in which you can open a file or folder.
HELP or **?**	Displays help texts and options.

To close a dialog box quickly, click on the box closing button.

Exiting Outlook

There are several methods for exiting Outlook.

- Click on **File**, then select **Exit**. This command allows you to exit Outlook while leaving e-mail connected (if you are already connected, of course).
- Click on **File**, then select **Exit and Log off**. This command allows you to exit Outlook and disconnect e-mail at the same time.
- Click on the system closing button on the title bar.
- Click on the system button located to the left of the title bar then select **Close**.

Executing commands

Outlook offers several possibilities for selecting commands, thus helping you to work faster.

Keyboard shortcuts

You can access a command using the keyboard without opening the menu bar. Throughout this book, at the end of each hour the keyboard shortcuts corresponding to the various commands or actions you have learned in the hour will be shown.

The drop-down menus display certain keyboard shortcuts (see Figure 1.8).

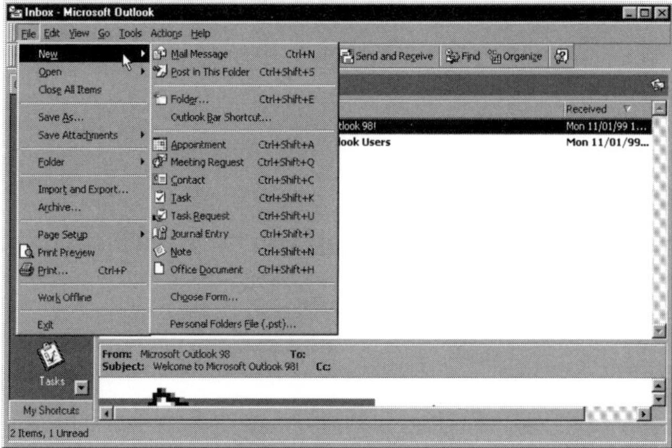

Figure 1.8: Keyboard shortcuts offered in the File menu

Help bubbles

Outlook, as well as all the other programs in the Office 97 suite, allows you to quickly see the information relating to a button, a command or an option, by means of help bubbles.

To display the help bubble for a button, move the mouse pointer onto the button concerned, then leave the pointer on it until the name of the button appears (see Figure 1.9).

Figure 1.9: Help bubble for the New Mail Message button

To display the help bubble for a dialog box option, click on the question mark then move the pointer onto the desired option.

*If the dialog box does not have a question mark, click on the option for which you want to display a help bubble, then press **Shift-F1**.*

Displaying using symbols

Working in Outlook is based on the principle of navigating between folders. To do this, Outlook displays information rapidly using symbols. At the end of each hour, a table will summarise those symbols you have just learned.

Table 1.5: Keyboard shortcuts in Hour 1.

Action	Keyboard shortcut
Open a menu	**Alt**-underlined letter
Select a command in a menu	Underlined letter of the desired command
Exit Outlook	**Alt-F4**
Confirm a dialog box	**Enter**
Cancel a dialog box	**Escape**
Display the help bubble for a command or an option in a dialog box	Move the pointer onto the command or option and press **Shift-F1**

Hour 2

Your first steps

The contents for this hour

- Outlook Bar
- Outlook Groups
- Folder List
- The Office Assistant
- Help
- Outlook Today

Outlook bar

Located on the left side of the screen, the Outlook bar allows you to navigate quickly between the folders (see Figure 2.1). As you saw in Hour 1, the different components of Outlook are organised as folders (Inbox, Tasks, Contacts, etc.). Using this bar you can select the folder you want to open. Outlook also offers the Folder List for navigating between the different components. This will be described later in this hour.

***Figure 2.1:** The Outlook Bar allows you to choose the folder you want*

If the Outlook Bar does not appear on your screen, click on **View**, then select **Outlook Bar** to display it.

The Outlook Bar displays icons, with the name of the corresponding folder beneath each one. These are shortcut icons. In addition, each folder containing one or more items (message, notes, etc.) displays the number of these items.

To open a folder, click on the shortcut icon of the desired folder.

Changing the size of the shortcut icons

To navigate in the Outlook Bar, click on the small arrows.

Because the shortcut icons are large, you cannot display all the folders. However, it is possible to choose smaller shortcut icons.

To choose small icons:

1. Move the pointer into the Outlook bar and right-click (see Figure 2.2).
2. Select **Small Icons**.

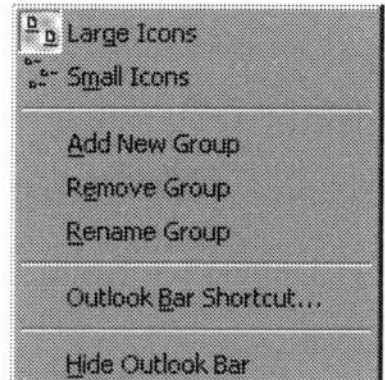

Figure 2.2: The context-sensitive Outlook bar menu

OUTLOOK GROUPS

In Figure 2.1, the Outlook Bar contains three groups of folders: the Outlook Shortcuts group, the My Shortcuts group and the Other Shortcuts group.

Here is a description of each of these groups:

- **Outlook Shortcuts.** Contains folders which allow you to work with the various functions, e.g. e-mail, the Calendar, Contacts and Notes;
- **My Shortcuts.** Contains folders which help you to manage, organise and categorise your sent or received messages; and
- **Other shortcuts.** Gives quick access to folders or files present in another application.

Accessing a group

The Outlook Shortcuts group is displayed by default. The other groups appear in the form of buttons in the lower part of the Outlook Bar.

To open another group, click on the button of the desired group (see Figure 2.3).

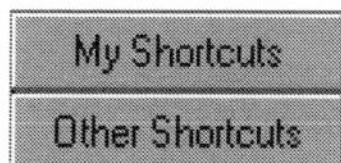

Figure 2.3: The buttons of the other groups in the Outlook Bar

Outlook Shortcuts Group

Displayed by default, the Outlook Shortcuts group gives direct access to the different work folders. You have already seen a description of them and what they allow you to do in Hour 1.

My Shortcuts Group

The My Shortcuts group helps to organise the management of your mail for messages both received and sent (see Figure 2.4). See Table 2.1 for a description of the folders in the My Shortcuts group.

Table 2.1: The functions of the folders in the My Shortcuts group.

Icon	Description
Inbox	Contains all messages received
Drafts (1)	Contains all the messages on which you are working

Figure 2.4: The bar of the My Shortcuts group

Other Shortcuts Group

The Other Shortcuts group gives direct access to the other applications or folders on your computer. This is particularly useful when you want to view or consult a file without leaving Outlook.

Folder List

Outlook provides another method of display, the Folder List. This allows you to display all your Outlook folders.

To display the Folder List, click on the name of the active folder in the view section (see Figure 2.5).

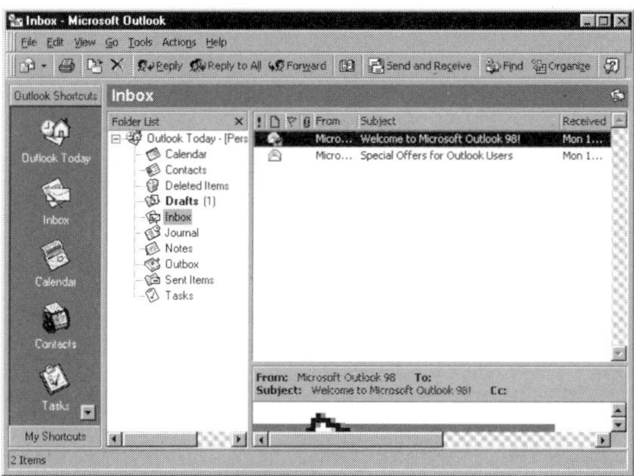

Figure 2.5: The Folder List

To open a folder from this list, click on it.

If you want to view the whole of the active folder in the right hand part of the screen while keeping the Folder List open, click on the button in the list which shows a pin.

To close the Folder List, double-click on the pin.

Creating a folder

To create a personal folder:

1. Click on the menu **File**, **New**.
2. Select **Outlook Folders** from the cascade menu.

   The Create Personal Folders dialog box is displayed (see Figure 2.6).
3. Click on the **Parent Folder** icon in the **Save in** field, then select the desired folder.
4. Click on **Create**.

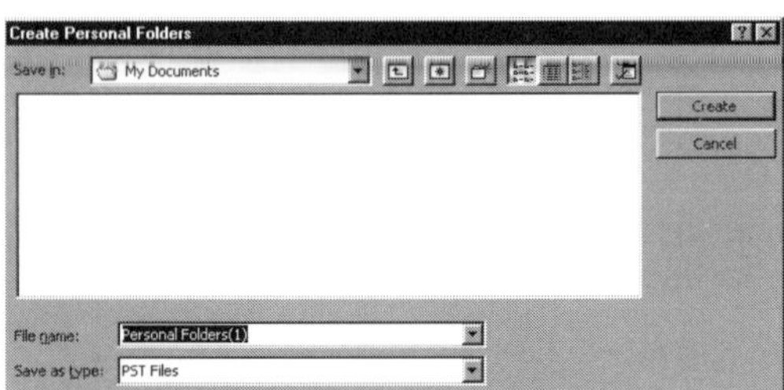

Figure 2.6: Creating your personal folder

To create a folder, click on the menu **File, New,** then select **Folder** in the cascade menu. In the box Create New Folder (see Figure 2.7), select the type of items to be contained in the new folder from the **Folder contains** field, then enter your name in the **Name** field. Don't forget to click on **OK**.

To create a sub-folder, follow the same procedure, but first click on the folder in which you wish to create the sub-folder.

When you create a folder or a sub-folder, Outlook automatically creates a shortcut icon in the active group.

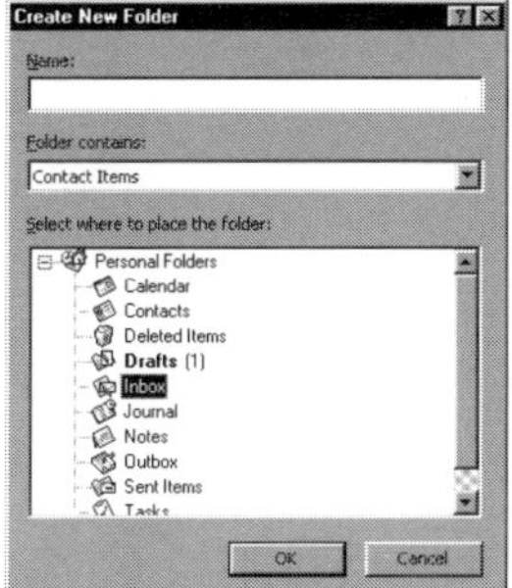

Figure 2.7: The Create New Folder dialog box

Deleting a folder

To delete a folder:

1. In the Outlook bar, right-click on the icon of the folder to be deleted to display its context-sensitive menu (see Figure 2.8).
2. Select **Remove from the Outlook Bar**.
3. Click on **Yes** in the dialog box requesting confirmation of the deletion.

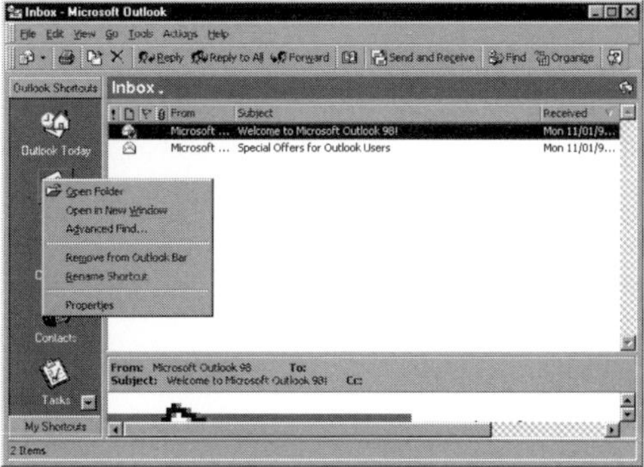

Figure 2.8: Context-sensitive menu of a folder

Office Assistant

Activating the Office Assistant

The Office Assistant must be active on the screen to be used.

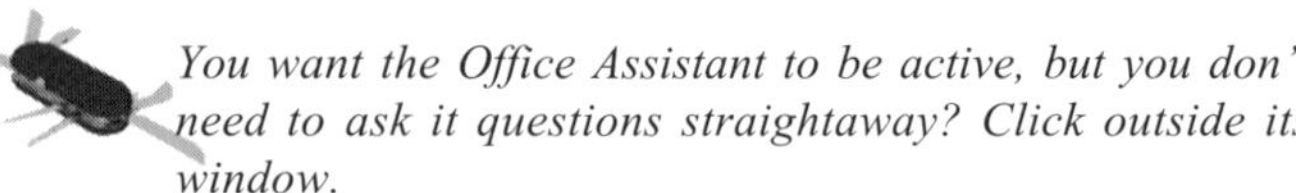

You want the Office Assistant to be active, but you don't need to ask it questions straightaway? Click outside its window.

There are several methods of displaying the Office Assistant (see Figure 2.9):

- click on the Office Assistant button in the Standard toolbar (at the extreme right);
- press **F1**; or
- click on the question mark in the toolbar then select **Help on Microsoft Outlook**.

Figure 2.9: The Office Assistant is displayed, ready to help you

The Office Assistant is common to all the programs in the Office suite. Any modifications you make to it will be carried over to the other programs. If the Office Assistant is active in Outlook, it will also be active in Word, Excel, etc.

To ask the Office Assistant questions:

1. If it is not active, click on the **Office Assistant** button in the Standard toolbar.
2. Select the desired subject from the list or enter your question in the highlighted text field (see Figure 2.10).

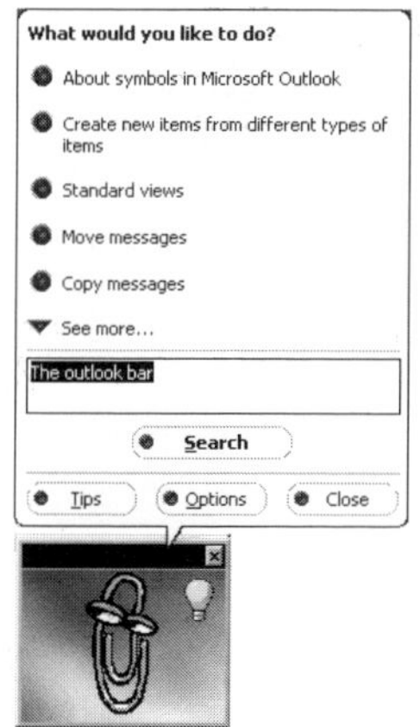

Figure 2.10: The Office Assistant offers a new list of topics

3. Click on **Search**.
4. Click on the topic of your choice in the new list displayed.

   The answer to your question is displayed in a help box.
5. When you have finished, click on the **Close** button in the help box.

Changing the appearance of the Office Assistant

Outlook allows you to customise the Office Assistant, to make it audible or to change its appearance.

To customise the Office Assistant:

1. After activating the Office Assistant, right-click on it.
2. Select **Choose an Assistant**.

   The Office Assistant Gallery box is displayed (see Figure 2.11).
3. Click on **Next** to scroll through the different Assistants.
4. Click on the **Options** tab.
5. Activate and/or deactivate the desired options.
6. When you've found the Assistant you like, click on **OK**.

Figure 2.11: Customising your Assistant

You may have to insert the Outlook 98 CD-ROM to display the list of available Assistants.

Help

Outlook has other methods for obtaining help. These are accessible via the question mark located in the menu bar.

The various types of help offered by Outlook (see Figure 2.12) are:

- **Microsoft Outlook Help.** This command activates the Office Assistant. You have just learned how to use it.
- **Contents and Index.** This command opens the Outlook help window, containing three tabs: Contents, Index and Find. Using these tabs, you can search in Help for a folder or a command.
- **What's This?** This command activates context-sensitive help for a button or a dialog box.

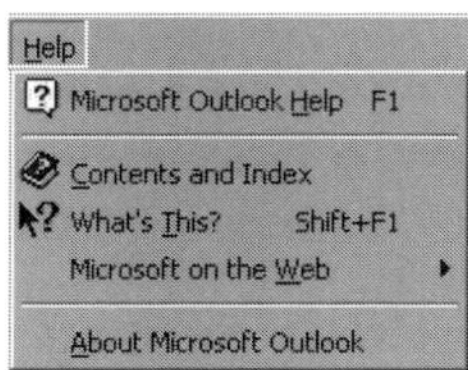

Figure 2.12: The different kinds of help available

Tip of the day

Another kind of help does not appear in this list; this is the Tip of the Day.

To display a Tip:

1. Click on the button representing a light bulb in the Office Assistant window.
2. When you have read the Tip, you can display another by clicking on **Next** or **Previous**.
3. When you have finished, click on **Close**.

Contents and Index

In the Contents and Index command, Outlook offers several tabs for different search functions.

The Contents tab

You can display the help boxes using the **Contents** tab. Each icon in the box represents a book containing chapters describing the items covered by the book. Keep this concept in mind for easy navigation.

To use help Contents:

1. Click on the **?** in the menu bar.
2. Select **Contents and Index**, then click on the **Contents** tab.
3. Double-click on the icon opposite the desired "chapter".
4. Double-click on the help topic of your choice.
5. When you have read the help topic, click on the **Close** button.
6. Click on the **Close** button of the Contents window.

When you consult a help window, certain buttons or symbols are displayed. Table 2.2 describes these different symbols or buttons. Refer to this table to refine your help search.

Table 2.2: The different symbols and buttons in the help box.

Symbol or button	Description
Button with two arrows	Indicates the procedure to be followed to execute a command
Button with arrow pointing upwards	Performs the procedure to be followed to execute a command
Button with a question mark	Opens a box containing more information on a command or procedure
Underlined words	A single click on this word gives the definition of the word

Using the Options menu in a help box, you can print the topic, make annotations, place bookmarks, copy the topic and format it.

The Index tab

The **Index** tab allows you to search, in alphabetical order, the functions of Outlook (Connection, Modem, etc.) and the actions which can be carried out (Insert, Copy and Paste, etc.).

To use the **Index** tab:

1. Click on the **?** in the menu bar.
2. Select **Contents and Index**, then click on the **Index** tab.
3. Enter the name of the action or the function you are searching for in field 1.

   In field 2, an alphabetical list will be displayed with the topic corresponding to the name you have entered highlighted.
4. Double-click on the topic selected. A dialog box may open to allow you to refine your search.
5. Double-click on the desired topic in the dialog box.
6. When you have finished, click on the **Close** button in the help box.
7. Click on the **Close** button in the Index.

The Find tab

The **Find** tab allows you to search more quickly by reducing the topics to be searched. You enter a word, and Outlook provides a list of close matches. You can choose to display the topic corresponding to the word or the topics for all the words suggested.

The following procedures indicate the approach to be followed when you use this tab for the first time. Subsequently, you need only repeat steps 1, 2, 5, 6, 7 and 8.

To use the **Find** tab:

1. Click on the **?** in the menu bar.
2. Select **Contents and Index**, then click on the **Find** tab.
3. Click on **Next**.
4. Click on **Finish**.
5. Enter the name of the command sought in field 1.

   Several close matches are displayed highlighted in field 2.
6. Click on the word that most closely matches your search.
7. Click on one of the topics displayed in field 3, then click on **Display**.
8. When you have finished, click on the **Close** button in the help window.
9. Click on the **Close** button in the **Find** tab.

The What's this? command

This command is very practical, because it displays an explanatory window on any item of your choice. It is context-sensitive help. To use it:

1. Click on the **?**, then select **What's this?**.
2. The pointer changes into a question mark with a black arrow. Place the pointer on the relevant button and click.

Outlook Today

To open this folder, click on the **Outlook Today** button in the Outlook Shortcuts bar. This folder allows you to quickly display appointments and meetings for the following five days, to quickly find a contact, to see whether you have received any new e-mail messages and to see what tasks you have to carry out.

Quickly find a contact

In Hour 3, you will learn how to create records for your contacts, but you can already search for a contact using the Outlook Today folder. Click in the text field located in the upper right hand part of the Outlook Today window (see Figure 2.13), then enter the name of the contact to search for. Finally, press **go** or click on **Find Now** (see Figure 2.14).

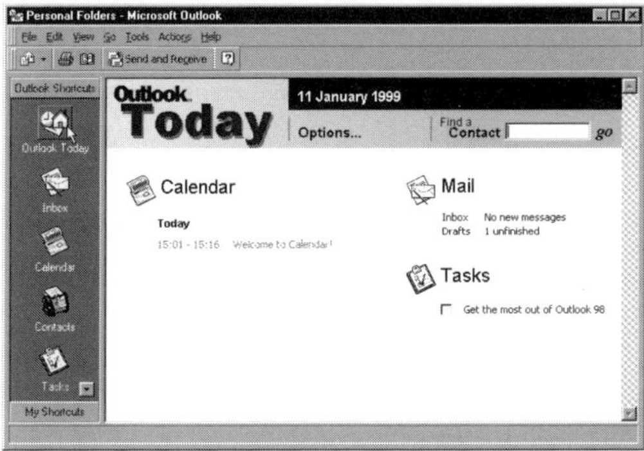

Figure 2.13: Outlook Today field allows quick searching for a contact

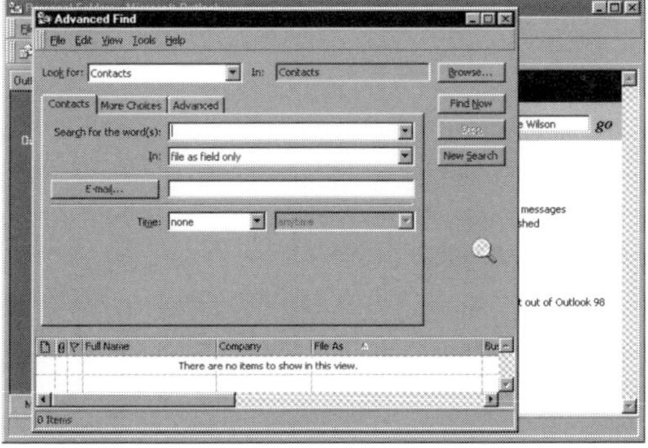

Figure 2.14: The required contact record appears

Customising the Outlook Today folder

Outlook allows you to quickly customise this folder. To access the different customising options, click on **Options** (see Figure 2.15).

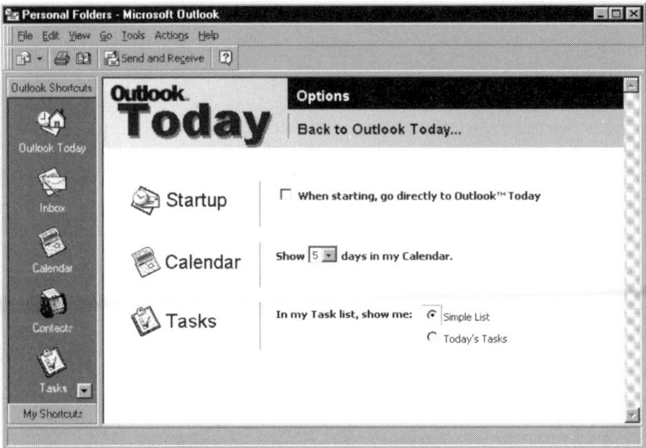

Figure 2.15: Customising Outlook Today

To quickly display your different tasks and appointments for the day, you can choose the normal display of this folder when Outlook is started. To do this, click on the option **On start-up, go direct to Outlook Today**.

If you want to display Calendar entries for a different number of days, click on the arrow in the **Display in my Calendar for X days** option, then choose the desired number of days.

You can choose to display the list of tasks for the day or a list of all the tasks to be carried out. To do this, click on the desired option in the **Tasks** field.

Finally, you can choose another type of style for this folder by clicking on the arrow of the **Display Outlook Today in this Style** option in the **Styles** field.

The choice of other styles is only accessible if you insert the Outlook CD-ROM in the drive.

To return to the folder, click on the **Return to Outlook Today** option.

Table 2.3: Keyboard shortcuts in Hour 2.

Action	Keyboard shortcut
New sub-folder	**Ctrl-Shift-E**
Activate Office Assistant	**F1**
Go to a folder	**Ctrl-Y**
Activate the What's this? command	**Shift-F1**
New folder	**Ctrl-Shift-E**

Hour 3

Contacts and the Address Book

The Contents for This Hour

- Contacts Folder
- Creating a contact
- Managing contacts
- Importing items
- Address Book

Contacts Folder

A contact is a person or a company with whom you communicate. These references are indexed in the Contacts Folder (see Figure 3.1). Click on **Contacts** in the Outlook Shortcuts bar to open this folder.

The Contacts Folder also allows you to:

- display all the contacts in several different views;
- classify the information relating to your contacts by their name, the name of their company, their town or other information such as their area of activity, etc.;
- consult discussions you have had or activities you have carried out with a particular contact through the **Journal** tab which is directly linked to this folder (see Hour 8);
- sort, filter or group your contacts;
- connect to the contact's Internet site (see Hour 12);
- plan meetings (see Hour 9); and
- automatically telephone a contact.

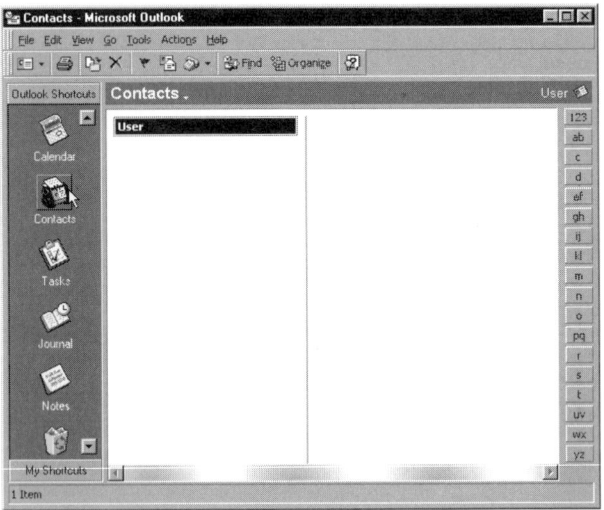

Figure 3.1: The Contacts Folder screen with its own toolbar

Standard toolbar of the Contacts Folder

Besides the buttons which are common to all toolbars, you will find the buttons which are specific to the Contacts toolbar described in Table 3.1.

Table 3.1: Buttons specific to the Contacts toolbar

Button	Description
	Opens a dialog box which allows you to create a contact. If you click on the small arrow, a drop-down list will open, allowing you to select another option.
	Allows you to print the item displayed.
	Allows you to quickly move a contact to another folder.
	Allows you to delete a contact.
Find	Allows you to quickly find a contact.
Organize	Allows you to customise this folder.

Figure 3.2: The toolbar of the Contacts folder

To activate a button in the toolbar, simply click on it.

Alphabetic tab

This tab allows you to directly access an existing contact by selecting the first letter of its name.

To find a Contacts record, click on the desired letter; the first contact starting with the selected letter is displayed on screen (see Figure 3.3).

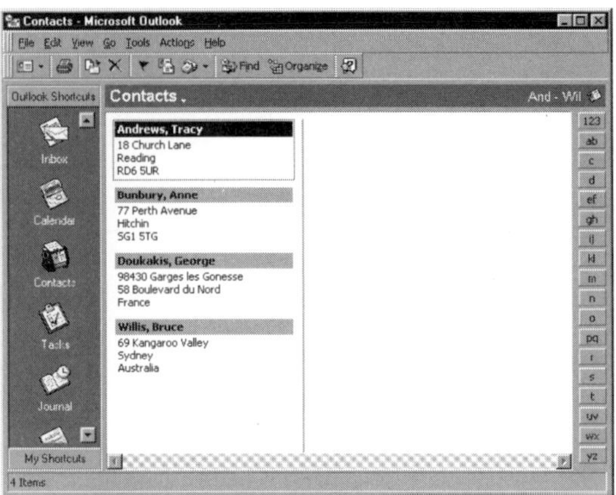

Figure 3.3: The screen displays the first Contacts record whose surname begins with A

CREATING A CONTACT

Use the New Contact button located on the extreme left of the Standard toolbar. It is a small open diary.

To create a contact:

1. Click on the **New Contact** button in the toolbar.

   A record form for entering information for a contact is displayed with its own specific toolbar (see Figure 3.4).

2. If necessary, click on the **General** tab (the other tabs are described later in this chapter).

3. Complete the fields of interest to you (see Table 3.2), remembering that it is essential to enter a name. After completing each field, press **Enter**.

4. Click on **Save and New** in the toolbar to open a new Contacts record or click on **Save and Close** in the toolbar if you do not want to enter another new Contacts record.

*If you want to exit a Contacts record without entering anything, click on **File**, then select **Close**.*

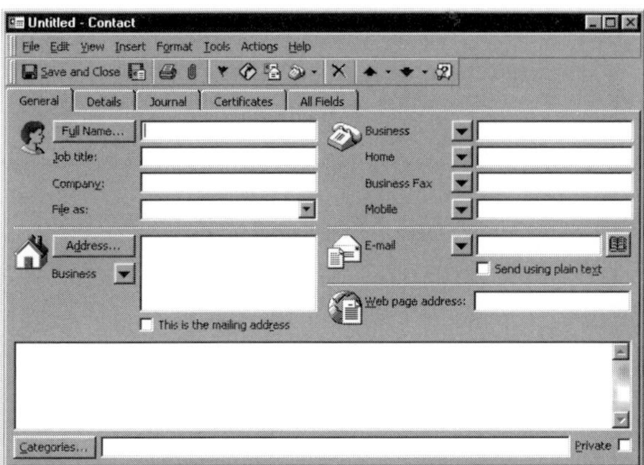

Figure 3.4: The Contacts record contains information about a contact

*To delete an Address Card (the default view format of a contact record), click on the Address Card, then press **Del**. You can also use the **Delete** button in the Standard toolbar.*

Table 3.2: Fields in the Contacts record and their functions.

Zone	Function
Full name	The name of the contact. Click on the **Full Name** button to enter the person's title, first and second names, surname and any suffix.
Company	The name of the company.

Table 3.2: Fields in the Contacts record and their functions (cont.).

Zone	Function
Address	The address of the contact. Click on **Address** to add address information (street name, city, postcode, etc.) in separate fields instead of all in the Address field
File as	Select the method by which to file the contact's names (last name first, first name first, by company, by town, county, etc.)
Telephones	The various telephone numbers for the contact
E-mail	The e-mail address of the contact
Web page address	The Web site address of the contact
Text field	Allows entry of notes or descriptions concerning the contact
Categories	Allows choice of a category from a list offered by Outlook. You can file your contacts by their business sector or other classification

To modify an Address Card, double-click on the title of the Address Card, then make your changes. Don't forget to save before closing the Contacts record.

Indicating a category

The category concept is very important; it is a keyword or an expression which helps to sort or easily find your contacts and to trace contacts with similar features. Outlook offers a number of categories: Personal, Competition, Strategies, Suppliers, Pending, International, etc.

To choose a category:

1. When entering or making changes to your contact, click on the **Categories** button (see Figure 3.5).

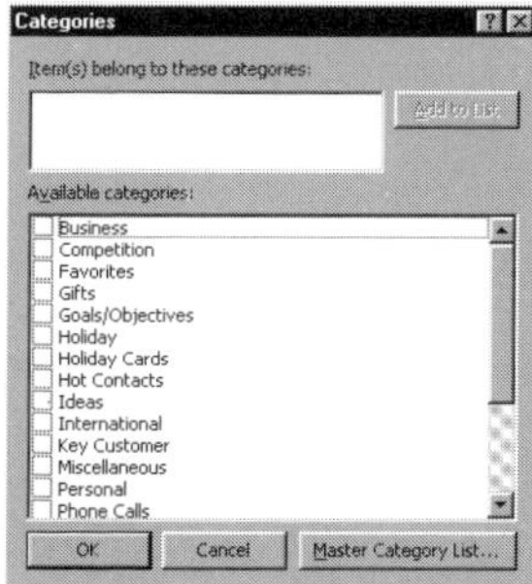

Figure 3.5: The Categories box

2. Click on the arrow in the scroll bar to scroll through the list.
3. Tick the box opposite the desired category.
4. Click on **OK**.
5. Click on **Save and Close** in the toolbar.

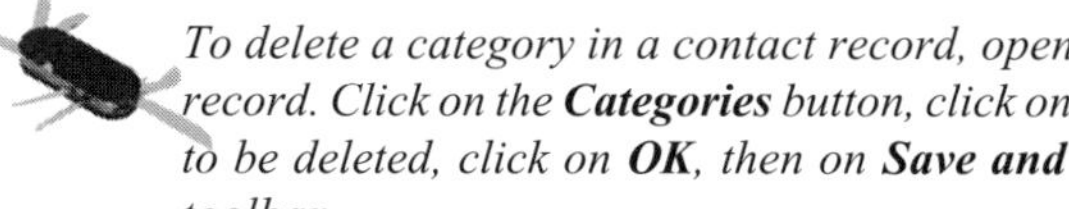

*To delete a category in a contact record, open the relevant record. Click on the **Categories** button, click on the category to be deleted, click on **OK**, then on **Save and Close** in the toolbar.*

To create a category, click on the **Organise** button in the Standard toolbar. In the window which is displayed, click on the option **Using categories**. Enter the name of the category to be created in the **Create a New Named Category** text field, then click on the **Create** button.

*To delete an existing category in any Contacts record, click on the **Categories** button. In the dialog box which is displayed, click on **Lists of Main Categories**. Click on the category to be deleted from the list, then click on the **Delete** button. Click on **OK** to confirm the deletion.*

If you have created all your Address Cards but have forgotten to indicate their category, instead of modifying the category for each record, you can use the Organiser option. Click on the **Organiser** button in the Standard toolbar. Click on the option **Using Categories**. Select the contacts to add to each category which you specify in the **Add Contacts...** option. Finally, click on the **Add** button.

Contact record tabs

The Contacts record has four tabs:

- **General.** See Table 3.2.
- **Details.** This allows you to indicate the contact's secretary/ assistant, birthday, surname, etc.
- **Journal.** This allows you to display Journal entries relating to the contact, if you have ticked the Automatically Save Entries box for the contact.
- **All fields.** This allows you to display all the fields provided by Outlook.

To use these tabs:

1. Click on the desired tab in the Contacts record.
2. Enter the relevant information and repeat the procedure shown for entering a contact.
3. When you have finished, click on **Save and Close** in the toolbar.

When you have deleted an item, e.g. an Address Card, click on the ***Deleted Items*** *button in the Outlook Shortcuts bar. The Address Card you have deleted appears (see Figure 3.6). To recover this Address Card, click on it, hold the mouse button down and drag it into the Contacts Folder in the Outlook Bar; it will then be restored.*

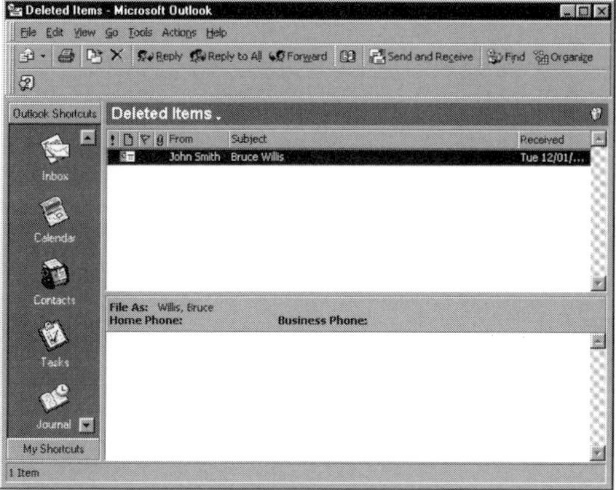

Figure 3.6: The Deleted Items folder stores items you have deleted

Displaying contacts

By default, contacts are displayed in the form of Address Cards (see Figure 3.7). To modify how your contacts are displayed, click on the **Display** menu, then select the desired type of display from the cascade menu.

If you want to modify the default display, click on the **Organise** button in the Standard toolbar. Click on the option **Using displays**, then select the desired default display from the list. Close the Ways of Organising Contacts window.

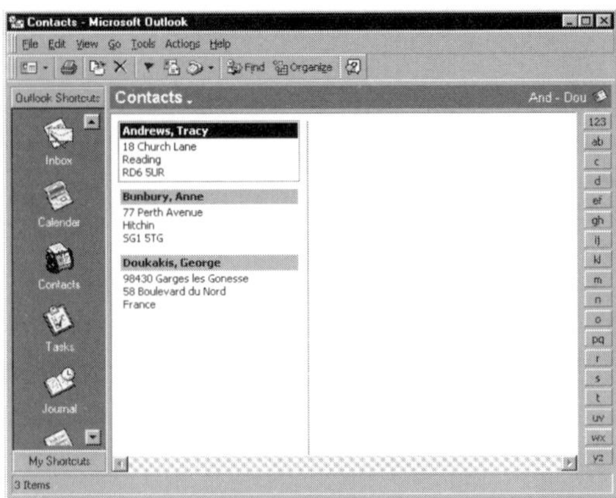

Figure 3.7: The contacts list in Address Cards format

Above, you can view the name, first name(s), full address and telephone number of each of your contacts, in the form of individual address cards. However, Outlook can also provide other types of display (see Table 3.3).

Table 3.3: The various displays available in the Contacts Folder.

Display	Description
Address Cards	Individual cards with addresses and telephone numbers
Address Cards (detailed)	Individual cards with addresses, telephone numbers and other details
Telephone list	List showing the company name, telephone and fax number
By category	List grouped by category and sorted by the name indicated in the **File As** field

Table 3.3: The various displays available in the Contacts Folder (cont.).

Display	Description
By company	List grouped by company with titles, names and telephone numbers
By location	List grouped by country showing company names, counties, countries and telephone numbers
By Follow Up Flag	List grouped by types of follow-up flag (see Hour 4)

Depending on the changes you have made, Outlook may open a dialog box asking whether you want to save the existing display settings before you change to another view. Click yes or no.

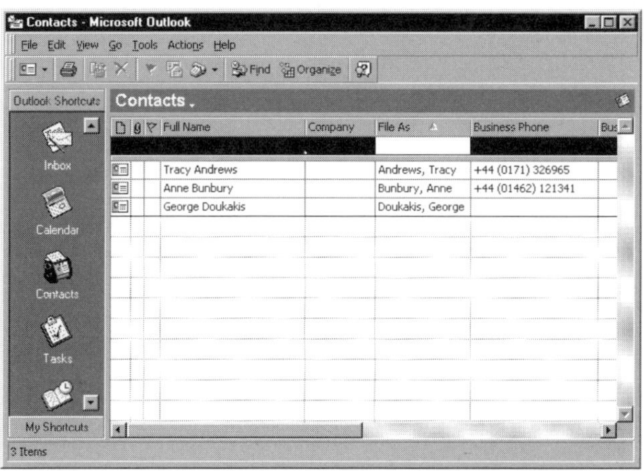

Figure 3.8: Your contacts displayed by telephone list

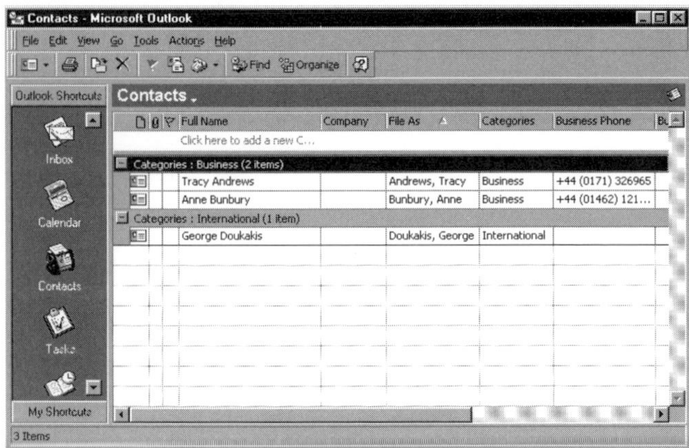

Figure 3.9: Your contacts displayed by category

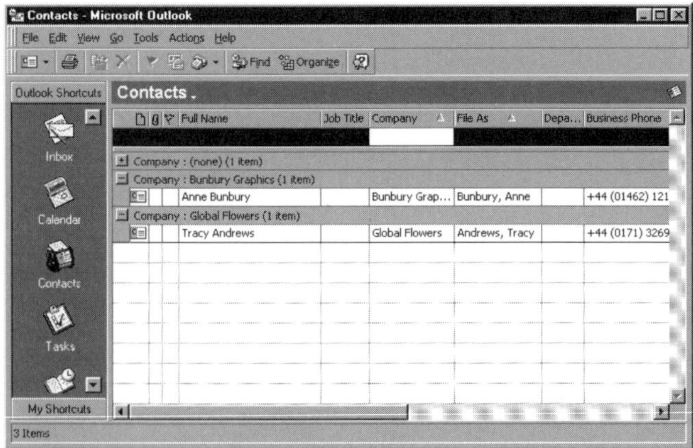

Figure 3.10: Your contacts displayed by company

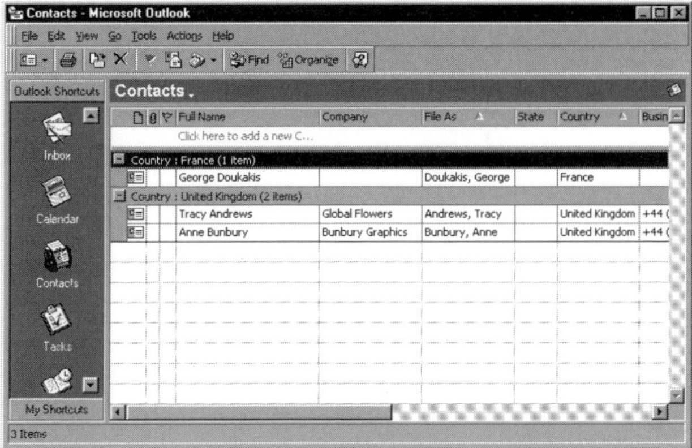

Figure 3.11: Your contacts displayed by location

MANAGING CONTACTS

Let's look now at the different possibilities offered for managing contacts.

Finding a contact

To find a contact:

1. Click on the **Find** button in the Standard toolbar.

   The upper part of the window displays the search screen and its options (see Figure 3.12).

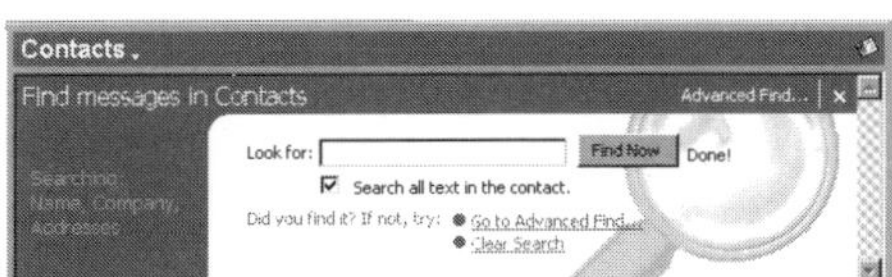

Figure 3.12: The window which allows you to search for items in the Contacts Folder

2. Enter the name of the contact (or other item) in the **Find** field.
3. Click on the **Find Now** button.

   The result of the search is displayed in the form of a table (see Figure 3.13).

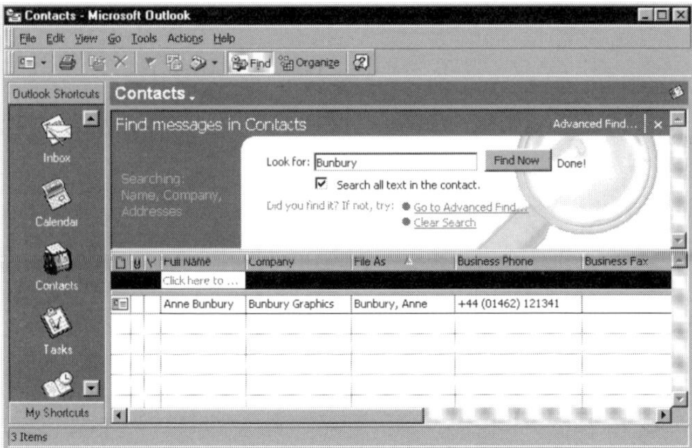

Figure 3.13: The result of your search is displayed in a table

4. Double-click on the button of the contact: the Contacts record is opened.
5. When you have finished, click on **File**, then select **Close**.
6. Click on **Close** in the Find section.

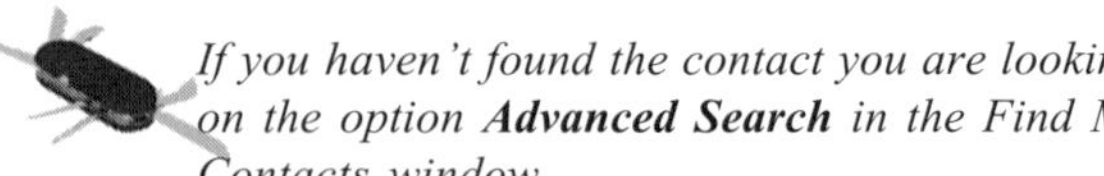

*If you haven't found the contact you are looking for, click on the option **Advanced Search** in the Find Messages in Contacts window.*

Moving a contact

If you want to move an Address Card to one of the Outlook folders, click on **Organise** in the Standard toolbar. In the window which is

displayed, click on the **Using the folders** option. From the list in the lower section, select the contact to be moved, then select the folder you want to move it to. Click on **Move**.

You cannot move a contact for which you have not entered an e-mail address.

Inserting a file in a contact

Outlook allows you to store, in a contact, all the items associated with the contact. For example, if you have sent a quote to your contact, you will store it in the contact; this, and other insertions, will allow you to record all dealings with this contact.

To insert a file in a contact:

1. Double-click on the title of the Address Card concerned.
2. Click on the **Insert File** button in the toolbar.
3. Choose your preferred drive and/or folder in the **Look in** field (see Figure 3.14).

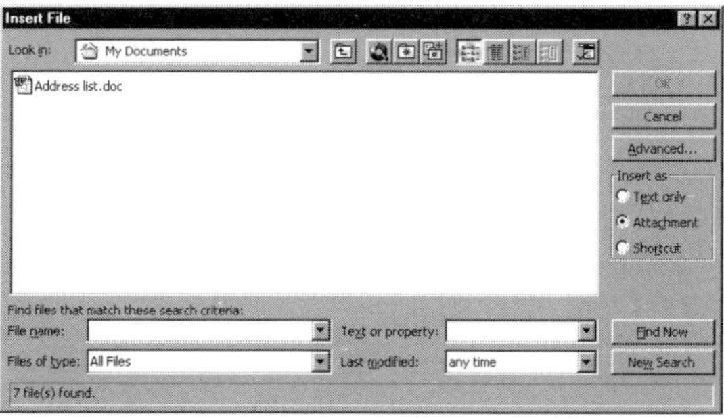

Figure 3.14: The Insert File box allows you to select a file to be inserted

4. Click on the file to be opened.
5. Click on **OK**.

The selected file is displayed in the text field of the Contacts record (see Figure 3.15).

Figure 3.15: The inserted file is displayed in the text field

*To delete a file inserted in an Address Card, double-click on the title. Click on the file icon and press **Del**, then click on **Save and Close**.*

Telephoning a contact

Outlook allows you to communicate directly with your contact. To do this, you must have an external modem or a modem card installed in your computer.

To telephone a contact:

1. After switching on your modem, click on the contact of your choice in the list of contacts; this can be done whatever the display mode.
2. Click on **Actions, Call Contact**.
3. From the cascade menu, select the telephone number displayed.
4. Click on the button **Start Call**.

5. Unhook your phone handset when you hear your contact's phone start to ring.
6. Click on the **Speak** button when your contact answers.
7. Click on **Hang Up** when you have finished your communication.
8. Click on **Close**.

IMPORTING ITEMS

You may already have a database of contacts stored in Access. During your installation of Outlook, you had the option to retrieve certain components. If you chose not to do this, you can still import them after installation.

Retrieving contacts from an Access database

To import items from Access:

1. Click on **File**, then select **Import and Export**.
2. Click on **Next**.
3. Click on **Microsoft Access** in the list, then on **Next** (see Figure 3.16).

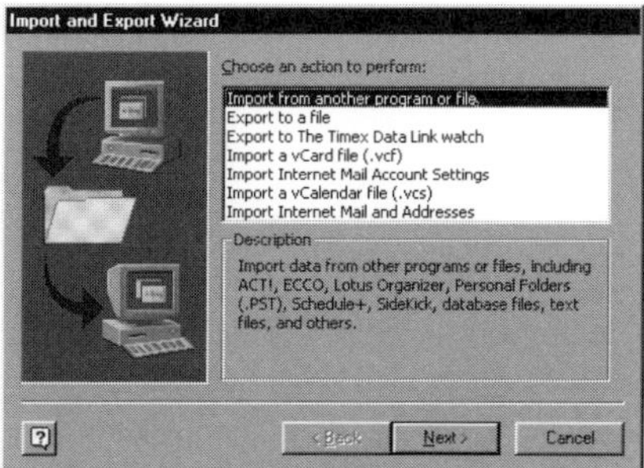

Figure 3.16: The importing items box

4. Enter the name of the file to be imported, then click on **Next**.
5. Click on **Contacts** in the list, then on **Next**.
6. Click on **Map Custom Fields.**
7. Click on the desired fields from the Microsoft Access list and hold down the button.
8. Drag to the Microsoft Outlook list and release the button.
9. Click on **Finish**.

Follow the same procedures for importing items from other Microsoft applications.

Address Book

To display the Address Book, click on **Tools**, **Address Book**.

When you want to send or reply to a message, you must use this Address Book. In Hour 4, you will learn how to send and receive e-mail messages.

The Address Book offers three types of address list:

- **Global Address List.** This list contains all the e-mail addresses of users within your company to whom you send messages. It is created and maintained by the network administrator for your company. You will see how to use it in Hour 4.
- **Contacts.** This is automatically created using the Contacts Folder. Any change to the e-mail address of a contact is automatically saved in this address list.
- **Personal Distribution List.** You create this list in order to group together people you contact often or to group your friends' e-mail addresses.

Creating your Personal Distribution List

It is very convenient to create a Personal Distribution List (or several of them) if you regularly send messages to a group of people. When you send the message, all you need do is select this distribution list rather than clicking on each person's name in turn to add them to your mailing list.

To create a Personal Distribution List:

1. Click on **Tools**, **Address Book** (see Figure 3.17).
2. Click on the **New Group** button.
3. Click on the **New Contact** button to create a new contact name or on the **Select members** button to select a group member from the existing list of contacts.
4. Repeat this procedure for each name to be inserted in the list.
5. Click on the **Close** button.

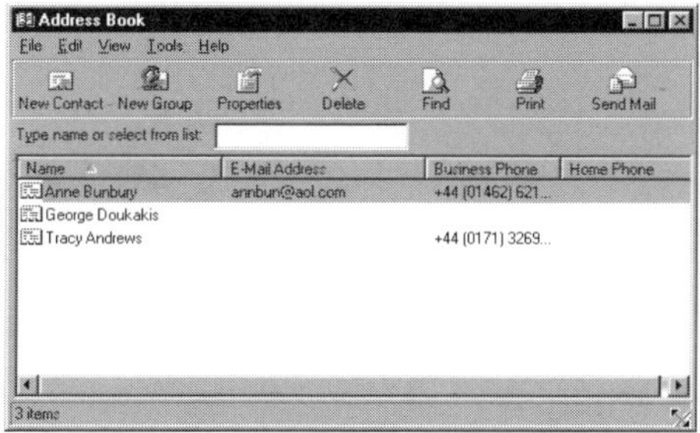

Figure 3.17: The Address Book dialog box

Deleting names from a Personal Distribution List

The Delete button (represented by an X) is located in the toolbar of the Address Book box.

To delete a Personal Distribution List:

1. Click on **Tools, Address Book**.
2. Click on the desired distribution list.
3. Click on the first name to be deleted, then click on **Delete** in the toolbar of the box.

4. Repeat this procedure for each of the names to be deleted from the Personal Distribution List.
5. Click on **File**, then select **Close**.

Table 3.4: Contacts folder symbols.

Symbol	Description
	Activities of the contact automatically recorded in the Journal
	Contact with enclosure

Table 3.5: Keyboard shortcuts in Hour 3.

Action	Keyboard shortcut
In the Contacts Folder	
New contact	**Ctrl-N**
Open contact record	Place the cursor on the contact and press **Ctrl-O**
Print a contact	Select the contact and press **Ctrl-P**
Copy	**Ctrl-C**
Paste	**Ctrl-V**
Delete	**Ctrl-D**
In a contact record	
Save	**Ctrl-S**
Close	**Alt-F4**
Find a contact	**F4**

Hour 4

Receiving messages

THE CONTENTS FOR THIS HOUR

- Inbox folder
- Setting up your e-mail system
- Receiving and reading messages
- Managing and formatting messages received
- Handling Attachments

INBOX FOLDER

When you start Outlook, by default the Inbox is displayed (see Figure 4.1). This folder is the Outlook electronic mail service, your "letter box". It allows you to send and receive mail of all kinds (such as pictures, graphics, files and text). These different types of mail are sent through a mail centre (for example, MsMail, Exchange, Notes or cc:Mail) which is located on your network server.

The network server is like a mail centre which centralises all the letter boxes of the users within your company; this is the "Intranet" concept which, unlike the Internet, only operates within a company.

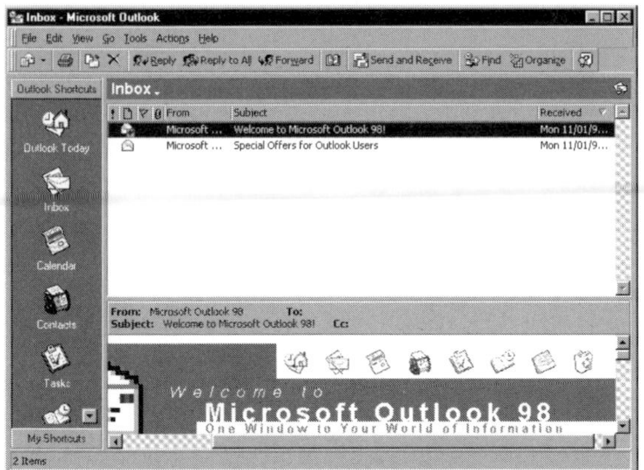

Figure 4.1: The Inbox folder screen with its toolbar

On first using Outlook, a welcome message may be displayed. To delete this, click on the message and press **Del**.

The Inbox folder standard toolbar

In addition to the buttons common to all standard toolbars, Table 4.1 lists the buttons specific to the Inbox standard toolbar.

Table 4.1: Buttons on the Inbox toolbar.

Button	Description
	Dialog box for sending a new message
Reply	Dialog box for replying to a message received
Reply to All	Dialog box for replying to all messages received
	Address Book

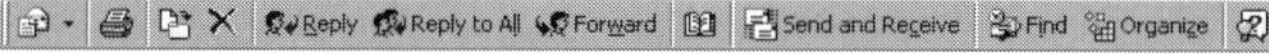

Figure 4.2: The Inbox folder's standard toolbar.

To activate an icon in the toolbar, simply click on it.

The Inbox indicators

Outlook displays a number of indicators as column headers in the **Message** field of the Inbox. In the columns below these indicators appear symbols, dates and text, allowing you to file and sort messages. Table 4.2 describes each of these indicators.

Table 4.2: The Inbox indicators.

Indicator	Description
	The importance of your message
	The status of the message: not read, read, saved
	The progress of the message: complete, not complete

Table 4.2: The Inbox indicators (cont.).

Indicator	Description
(paperclip icon)	This shows if there are files attached to the message
From	Sender of the message
Subject	Subject of the message
Received	Date of receipt of the message

*You can delete a message indicator; to do this, double-click on the message concerned, click on **Message Indicator,** then select **Erase**.*

SETTING UP YOUR E-MAIL SYSTEM

To allow Outlook to act as an e-mail service – receiving and sending messages – you must set certain parameters. The following procedures show how to set up an Internet e-mail account for a private individual. For companies, it will normally be the network administrator who configures PCs to manage e-mail.

To configure your e-mail system:

1. Click on **Tools**, **Accounts**.

   The Internet Accounts dialog box is displayed.

2. Click on the **Mail** tab.
3. Click on the **Add** button.
4. Click on **Mail** in the menu.

   The Internet Connection Wizard is displayed (see Figure 4.3).

5. In the **Display name** field, enter your name.
6. Click on the **Next** button.

   The second Internet Wizard dialog box is displayed.
7. Enter your e-mail address in the relevant field (this address will have been provided by your Internet Service Provider).
8. Click on the **Next** button.

   The third Internet Wizard dialog box is displayed.
9. Select your incoming mail server (normally POP3).
10. Enter the name of the incoming mail server (see your Internet Service Provider details).
11. Enter the name of the outgoing server mail (see your Internet Service Provider details).
12. Click on **Next**.
13. In the new dialog box, enter the name of the POP account in the relevant field and your password (provided by the Internet Service Provider).
14. Click on **Next**.
15. In the new dialog box, enter the desired name for your Internet e-mail account (your choice).
16. Click on **Next**.
17. Choose the desired type of connection in the new dialog box. This is normally the option **Connection Using My Phone Line**.
18. Click on **Next**.

    You must create or select a remote connection. Using this connection you will be able to connect to your Internet Service Provider.
19. Select your choice or click on **Create a New Remote Access Connection** (see Hour 12).

20. Click on **Next**.
21. You have now completed your connection to the Internet; click on the **Finish** button.

    Your account has been created in the Internet Accounts dialog box; click on **Close**.

In the standard toolbar, a new button is displayed: **Send and Receive**.

Figure 4.3: The first dialog box of the Internet Connection Wizard

Customising your e-mail

Outlook offers all sorts of options for managing your e-mail. Most of these options are grouped together in the Tools, Options dialog box.

To customise your e-mail system, click on **Tools, Options**. In the **Preferences** tab, click on the **E-mail Options** button (see Figure 4.4). Tick the desired options to activate them; untick the options not required to deactivate them. For more advanced options, click on the **Advanced E-mail Options** button (see Figure 4.5). Choose the options to be activated or deactivated, then click on **OK**.

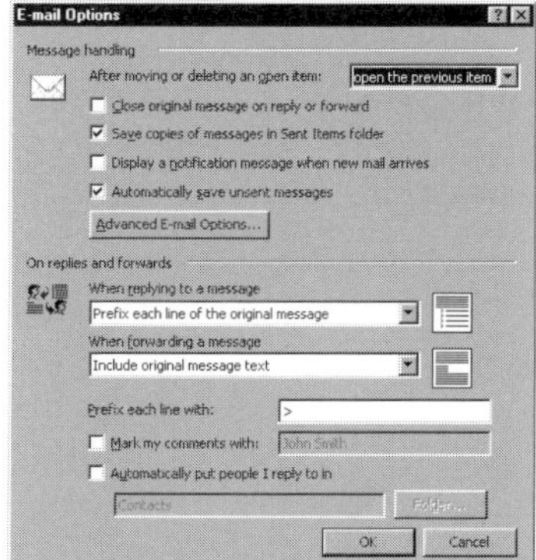

Figure 4.4: E-mail options

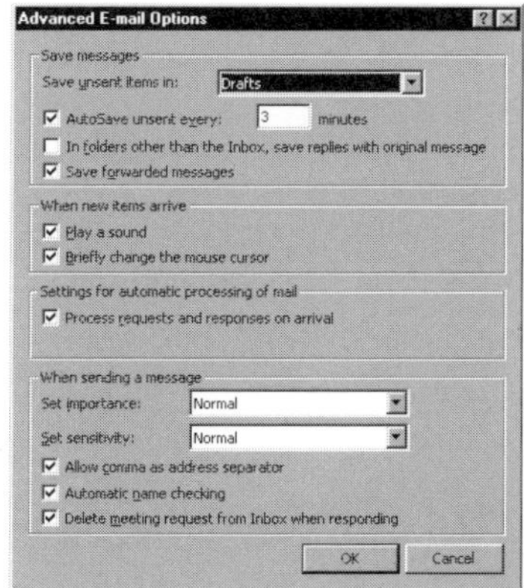

Figure 4.5: Advanced E-mail options

Receiving and reading messages

When you start Outlook, you will see messages which have arrived in the Inbox display field. If this box is empty, click on **Sending and Receiving Messages**. Outlook connects to the Internet, then displays the messages which have been received.

Figure 4.6: The Inbox displays a list of your messages

When you work on your computer, in whatever application, Outlook can let you know of the arrival of new messages (see Figure 4.7).

To set this up:

1. Click on **Tools**, then select **Options**. Click on **E-mail Options**.
2. Tick the option box **On Arrival of New Mail, Display a Warning Message**.
3. Click on **OK**.

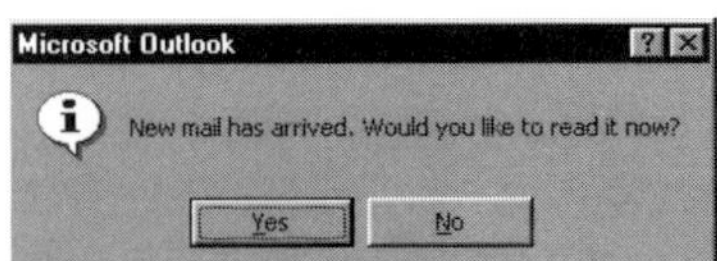

Figure 4.7: Message telling you that you have new mail

To read a message:

1. Double-click on the message you want to read (see Figure 4.8).
2. Click on the **Close** button when you have finished.

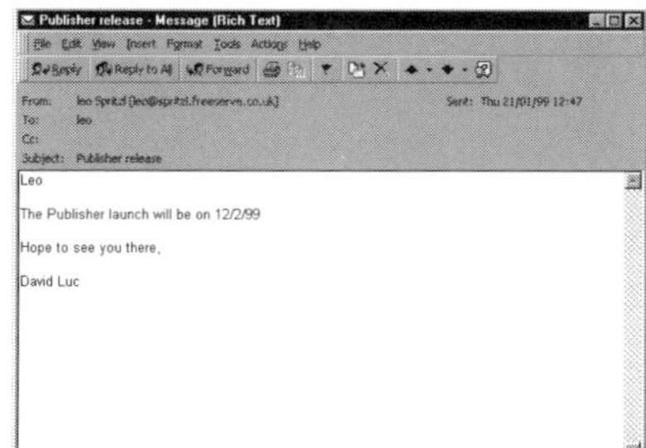

Figure 4.8: The Message box is displayed

To separate messages you have read from ones you have not, Outlook displays non-read messages in bold type, preceded by a closed envelope, and all read messages in ordinary type, preceded by an opened envelope.

To manually mark a message as read:

1. Click on the message concerned to select it.
2. Right-click (see Figure 4.9).
3. Select **Mark as Read**.

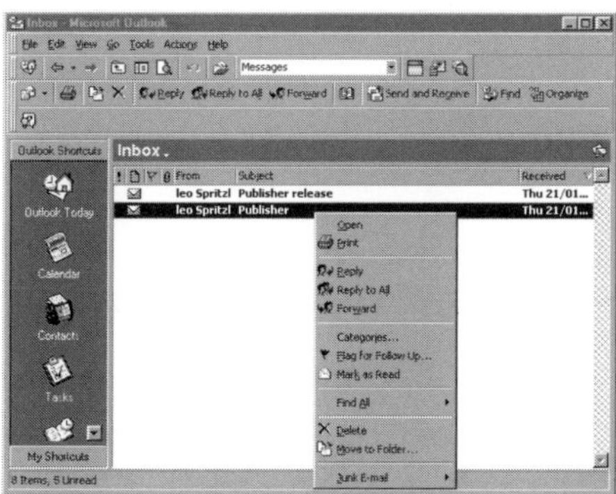

Figure 4.9: The context-sensitive menu for a message

You can also mark a message as not read directly in the message; click on **Edit**, then select **Mark as Not Read**.

*To mark all messages as read, click on **Edit** in the Inbox folder, then select **Mark All As Read**.*

To close the box displaying a message, click on **File**, then **Close**.

Displaying messages

As in the other folders, Outlook allows you to change the Inbox view using the command **Current View** in the **View** menu.

Among the views offered are:

- **Messages.** Default view in the form of a table in which the items appear in rows and columns. This is displayed in date order, with messages received most recently at the top of the screen.
- **Messages with partial view.** Displays the first line of the message in the Inbox.
- **Non-read messages.** Displays all messages which have not been read or which are marked as non-read.
- **Last seven days.** Displays all the messages received during the last week.
- **By sender.** Displays messages sorted by sender.
- **By topic.** Displays messages sorted by subject.

To display messages without opening them, click on **View**, then select **Preview Pane**.

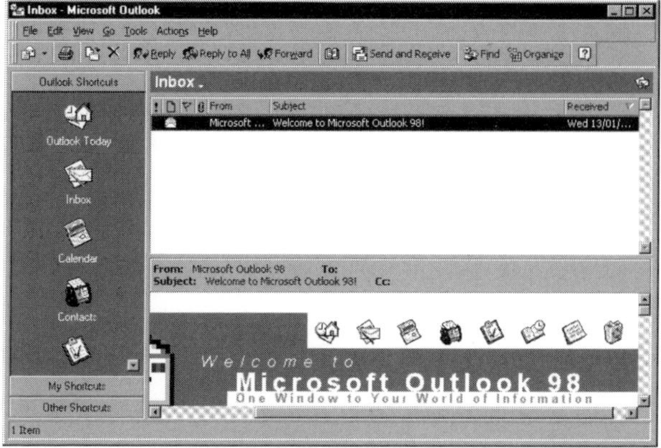

Figure 4.10: This function allows you to display the message in the Inbox without opening it

MANAGING AND FORMATTING MESSAGES RECEIVED

When you receive messages, different functions are accessible via the toolbar.

Reply or Reply to All

You use the buttons **Reply** or **Reply to All** on the Inbox folder toolbar. They show, respectively, a little man with an arrow and two little men with an arrow.

To reply to a message:

1. Click on the message concerned to select it.
2. Click on the **Reply** button in the toolbar.

   A dialog box opens, displaying the addressee (sender of the message) and the content of the original message is displayed in the text field (see Figure 4.11).

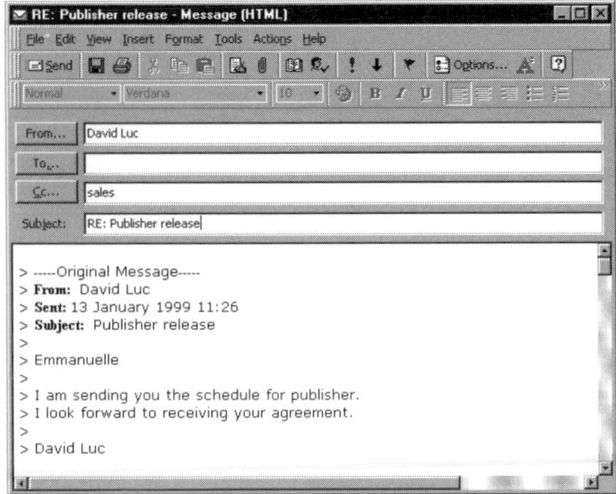

Figure 4.11: The dialog box for replying to a message

3. Type your answer in the text field, above the message received.
4. Click on **Send** in the toolbar.

*When you receive a message which has been copied to other people (shown in the **Cc** field), you may want to reply to the sender of the message and to all the people who received a copy of it. Simply follow the reply procedure shown above, but this time click on **Reply to All** instead of **Reply**.*

Forwarding a message

To forward a message, use the **Forward** button in the Inbox toolbar. It shows a little man and an arrow.

Sometimes you may receive a message by mistake. You must transfer it to the correct addressee, or you may want to send a copy of the message to someone else. You can add a note to the copy by entering it in the text field of the Message box.

To forward a message:

1. Click on the message concerned to select it.
2. Click on **Forward** in the toolbar (see Figure 4.12).

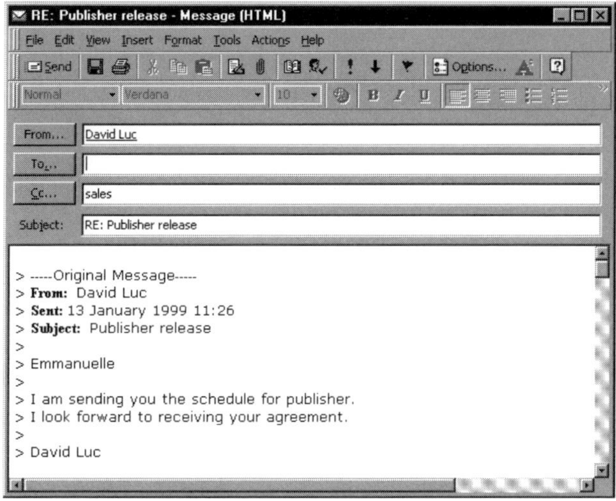

Figure 4.12: The dialog box for forwarding a message

3. Enter the name of the addressee in the **To** field.
4. If required, enter the name of the person to receive a copy of the message in the **Cc** field.
5. Enter the subject of the message in the **Subject** field.
6. Enter any required message in the text field.
7. Click on **Send** in the toolbar.

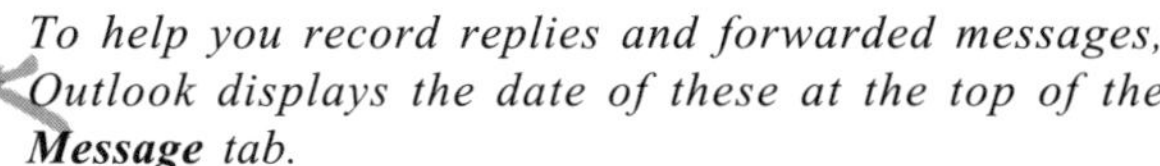

To help you record replies and forwarded messages, Outlook displays the date of these at the top of the ***Message*** *tab.*

Copying or moving a message to a folder

Several messages may arrive for you each day. Some will be deleted, others will be moved to their own specific folder. For example, you might receive a message for a contact or a task. You will have to store it in the relevant folder. You may also want to keep a message and copy it to another folder.

To copy a message:

1. Click on the message to be copied.
2. Click on **Edit**, then select **Copy**.
3. Click on the desired folder in the Outlook Shortcuts bar.
4. After opening the contact or the task, place the pointer in the text field and click on **Edit**, then select **Paste**.
5. Click on **Save and Close**.

To move a message:

1. Select the message to be moved. If you want to choose several, click on the first message, press **Ctrl**, hold it down, then click on the second message, and so on.
2. Click on the **Organise** button.
3. Click on the **Using Folders** option.
4. In the Move the Message option, click on the arrow, then select the desired folder.
5. Select the folder, then click on **OK** in the Select a Folder box.
6. Click on the **Move** button.

   If you have chosen Contacts, Outlook opens the Contacts record and inserts the message there. Otherwise, it opens the folder and inserts the message there.

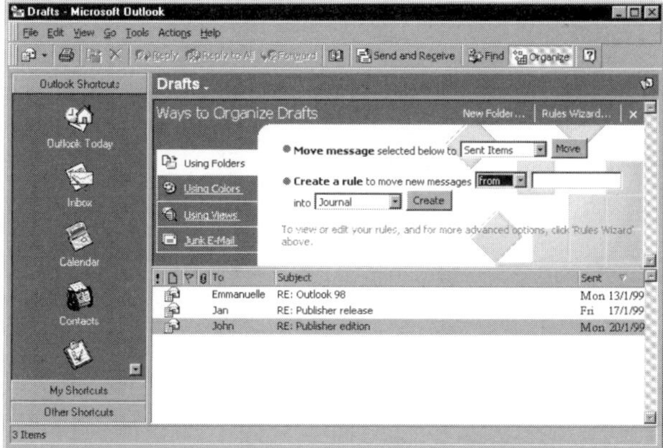

Figure 4.13: The window for organising your messages

Printing a message

Hour 11 contains all the page layout and configuration options for printing.

To print massages, click on the **Print** button in the Inbox toolbar, which shows a little printer.

To print a message:

1. Click on the message to be printed to select it.
2. Click on **Print** in the toolbar.

If you are in the Message box:

1. Click on **File**, then **Print**.

   The Print dialog box is displayed (see Figure 4.14).

2. Click on the **Copies** arrow and select the desired number of copies.
3. Click on **OK** to start printing.

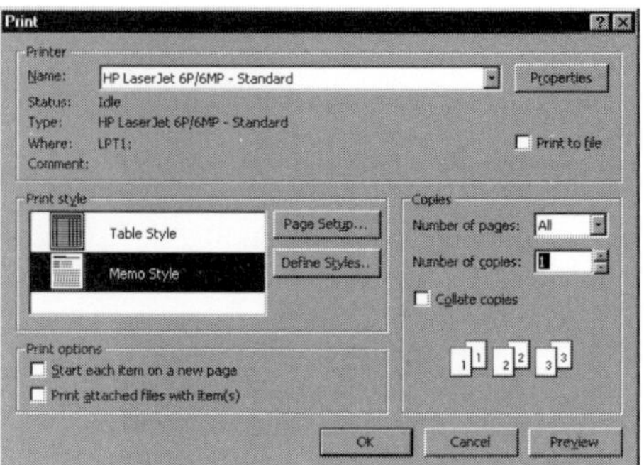

Figure 4.14: The Print dialog box

To delete a message in the Inbox, click on the message concerned and click ***Delete****.*

Grouping and sorting messages

If you don't want to delete or move your messages but you do want to sort them, you can do this.

There are two ways of managing your messages:

- **Grouping.** You can group all the messages concerning a particular item by sender or by subject. All these messages will be grouped in a table.
- **Sorting.** You can arrange the messages in ascending or descending date order, or in alphabetical order according to the senders' names.

To group messages:

1. Locate the pointer on the indicator you want to use for grouping your messages and right-click (see Table 4.3).
2. Select **Group By This Field** (see Figure 4.15).
3. Click on the + button to open the list grouped under this field.

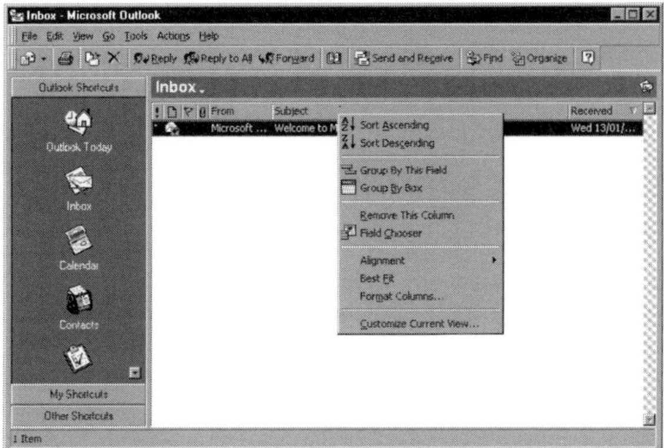

Figure 4.15: The context-sensitive menu for the indicators

*To ungroup the items, locate the pointer on the relevant indicator and right-click; select **Do Not Group By This Field**.*

Table 4.3: The different ways of grouping available items in the indicator bar

Indicator	Description
	By order of importance
	By message progress (complete, not complete)
Subject	By message subject
Received	By date of receipt

To sort messages, simply click on one of the available indicators (see Figure 4.16).

Figure 4.16: Sorting messages

Handling attachments

You will often receive messages containing an attachment: a file, a picture, or a graphic. They are identified by a paperclip symbol. Attachments are shown in the message in the form of an icon in the text field.

To display an attachment in a message:

1. Double-click on the attachment to open it using its own application program.
2. Click on **File**, then select **Close** to close the application and return to the message.

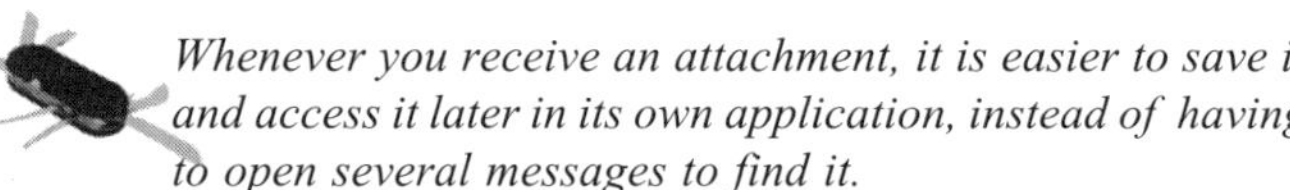

Whenever you receive an attachment, it is easier to save it and access it later in its own application, instead of having to open several messages to find it.

To save an attachment:

1. Within the message, click on the attachment, then **File**, then select **Save Attachment** (see Figure 4.17).

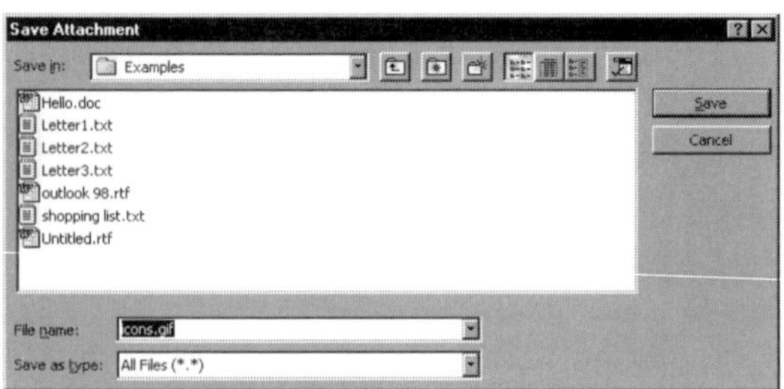

Figure 4.17: The Save Attachment dialog box

2. The name of the attachment is displayed in the **File name** field; enter a new name in this field if required, and click on **Save** after selecting the folder in which you want to save it.
3. In the Message box, click on **File**, then select **Close**.

Table 4.4: Inbox folder symbols.

Symbol	Description
	Message read
	Message not read
	Message of high importance
	Message of low importance
	Message with attachment
From	Group or sort by sender
	Group or sort by state of progress of the message
Subject	Group or sort by subject of the message
Received	Group or sort by date of receipt
	Sort by attachment

Table 4.5: Keyboard shortcuts for Hour 4.

Action	Keyboard shortcut
After selection	
Reply to a message	**Ctrl-R**
Forward a message	**Ctrl-F**
Delete a message	**Ctrl-D**
Open a message	**Ctrl-O**
Print a message	**Ctrl-P**
In the Message box	
Delete a message	**Ctrl-D**
Save a message	**Ctrl-S**
Send a message	**Ctrl-Enter**
In the Inbox	
New message	**Ctrl-N**
Verify the arrival of new mail	**F5**

Hour 5

Sending and managing outgoing messages

The contents for this hour

- My Shortcuts group
- Creating and sending messages
- The Deleted Items folder
- Managing and configuring outgoing messages

My Shortcuts group

This group was described in Hour 2.

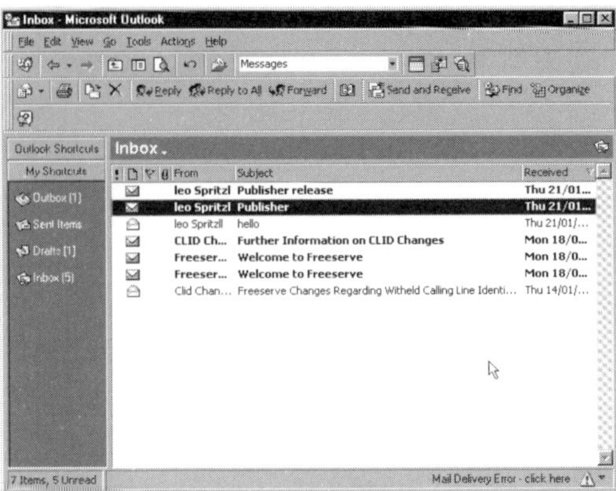

Figure 5.1: The screen of the My Shortcuts group

Standard toolbar of the My Shortcuts group

The toolbar is common to all the folders of the My Shortcuts group and is identical to that of the Inbox. See Table 4.1 for a description of the icons it contains.

The message flags

These are accessible in the Message box, and allow you to mark messages using different options. They are very useful, and are indicated by a red flag and a legend opposite the message when your addressee receives it.

To access the flag, you use the menu **Actions**, **Message Flags**.

The different indicators available are:

- Call;
- Do not Forward;
- Follow Up;

- For Your Information;
- Forward;
- No Response Necessary;
- Read;
- Reply;
- Reply to All; and
- Review.

We shall look at how these are used later.

Creating and sending messages

Everything to do with creating messages can be carried out either in the Inbox folder of the Outlook Shortcuts group, or in the My Shortcuts group.

Creating a message

You can send a message to anyone who has an e-mail address (see Hour 4) using the **New Message** button located at the extreme left of the Inbox toolbar.

To create a message:

1. Click on **My Shortcuts** in the Outlook Bar, then click on **Inbox**.
2. Click on **New Message** in the toolbar (see Figure 5.2).
3. Click on **To** (see Figure 5.3).
4. Select the desired Address Book.

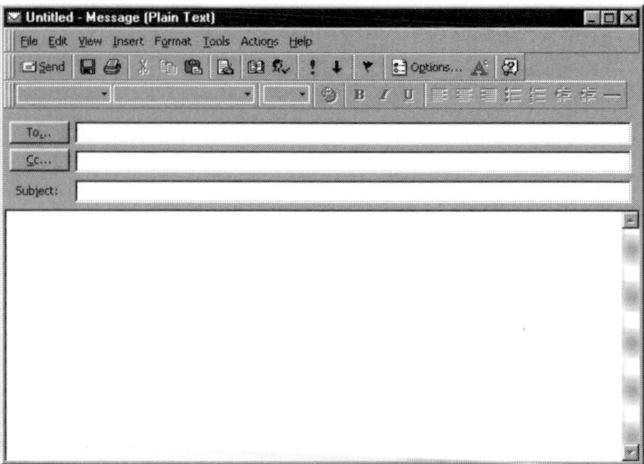

Figure 5.2: The Message box is displayed

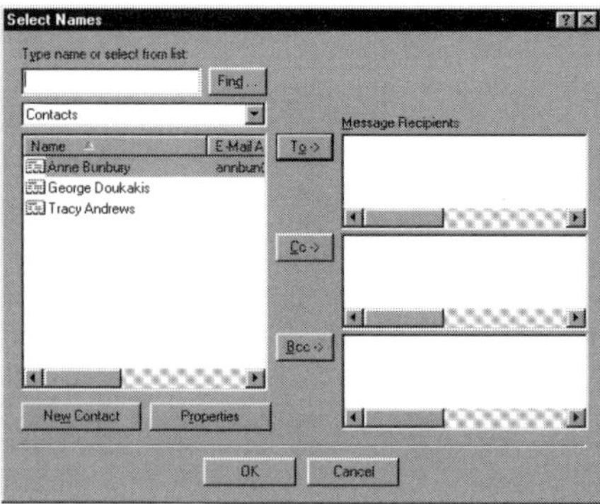

Figure 5.3: The Select Names box is displayed

5. Click on the name of your choice from the list on the left. Click on **To** to display it in the Message Recipients (To) list. Click on **Cc** to display it in the Message Recipients (Carbon Copy) list. Click on **Bcc** to display it in the Message Recipients (Blind Carbon Copy) list. Repeat this procedure for each of the people concerned.

*When you press the **Bcc** button, Outlook will send a confidential copy of the message to a person whose name will be 'blind' (invisible) to the other addressees.*

6. Click on **OK**.
7. In the **Subject** area, enter the subject of your message.
8. In the text field, enter the text of your message.
9. If you want to mark your message, click on **Actions, Flag for Follow Up**. Click on the arrow of the **Flag To** drop-down list, select the indicator of your choice, and click on **OK** (see Figure 5.4).
10. Click on **Send** in the Message box toolbar.

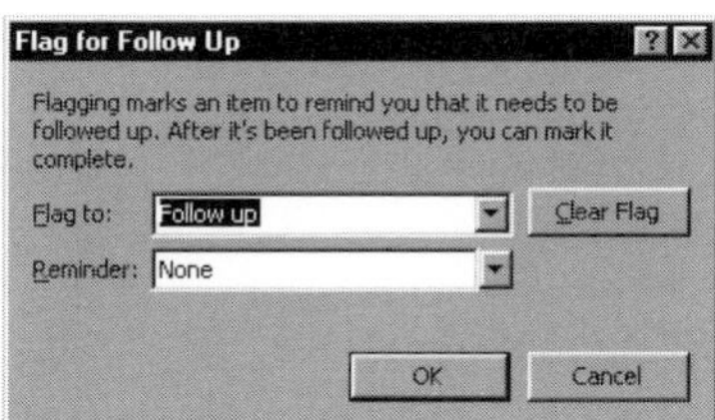

Figure 5.4: The Flag for Follow Up box is displayed

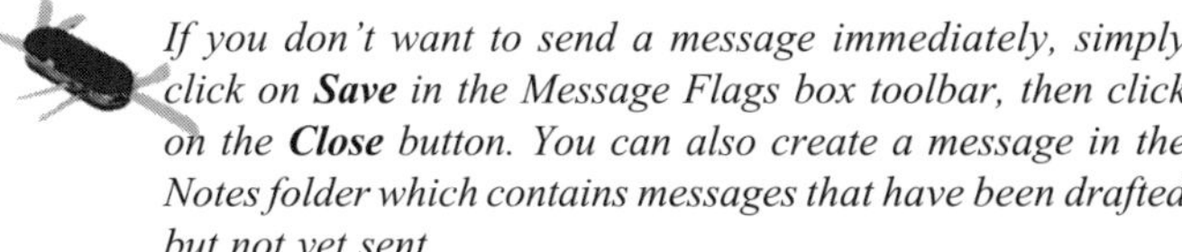

*If you don't want to send a message immediately, simply click on **Save** in the Message Flags box toolbar, then click on the **Close** button. You can also create a message in the Notes folder which contains messages that have been drafted but not yet sent.*

If you are connected to the Internet, Outlook will immediately send your message. If you are not connected, it stores your message in the Outbox folder. To send the stored message, open the Outbox folder, click on the message concerned, then click on **Send and Receive** in the standard toolbar. Outlook connects to the Internet and sends the message.

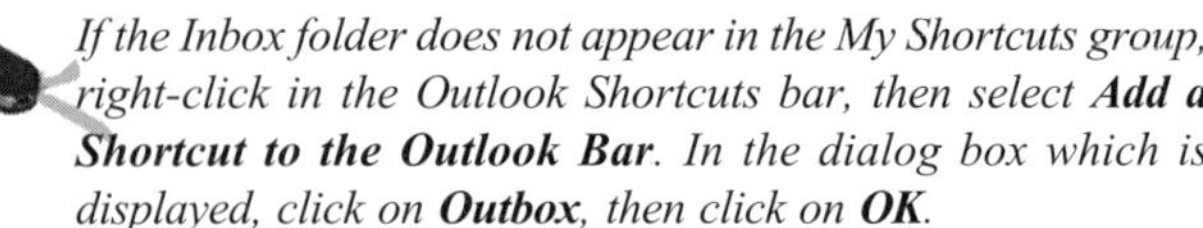

*If the Inbox folder does not appear in the My Shortcuts group, right-click in the Outlook Shortcuts bar, then select **Add a Shortcut to the Outlook Bar**. In the dialog box which is displayed, click on **Outbox**, then click on **OK**.*

After being sent, your messages are stored in the Sent Items folder.

If Outlook is unable to send your message (due to an incorrect e-mail address, bad connection, etc.), it displays an error message in the status bar. Click on it to open the dialog box and resend your message.

To return to a message, whether it has been sent or not, simply double-click on it.

If your addressee is not included in your address book, you must add the addressee's name to your Personal Distribution List. To do this, refer to the section on the Address Book in Hour 3. Don't forget, you can only send messages by using the Internet, i.e. to e-mail addresses.

The Options button in the Message box

This button allows you to configure certain options for the message which you are drafting (see Figure 5.5). To activate an option, click in its box or click on the arrow of the drop-down list and select your choice.

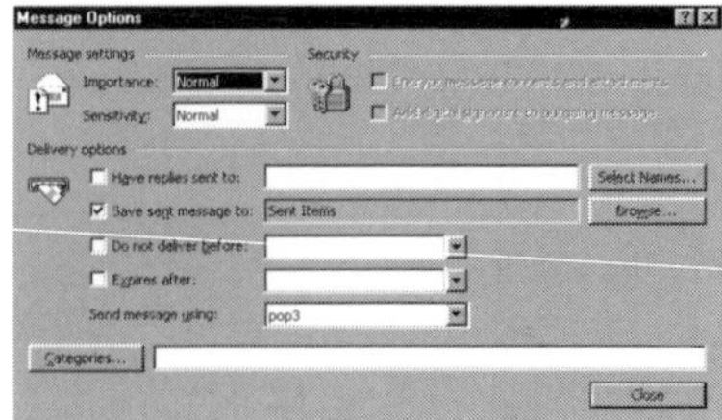

Figure 5.5: The Message Options dialog box

Table 5.1: The different options offered by the Options button of the Message box.

Option	Description
Have replies sent to	Sends replies to the message directly to another person
Importance	Defines the importance of the message
Sensitivity	Defines the distribution of the message
Save sent messages to	Sends a copy of this message to the folder indicated
Do not deliver before	Indicates the desired despatch date; a click on the arrow opens a calendar
Expires after	Indicates an expiry date for the message; a click on the arrow opens a calendar
Categories	Specifies a category for the message. A category is a key word or expression which helps to sort or easily find your messages (i.e. you can sort into suppliers, customers, competitors)
Tell me when this message has been read	Asks for acknowledgment that the message has been read
Tell me when this message has been delivered	Asks for acknowledgment that the message has been received

The options defined in a Message box only concern that message. To configure some of these options for all messages, click on ***Tools****, then select* ***Options****. Click on* ***E-mail options****, make your choices and click on* ***OK****.*

Signing a message

You can create a signature for your messages, which you can activate when you create messages. To create a signature, click on **Tools**, **Options**. Click on the **Mail Format** tab. Click on **Signature Selection**. In the dialog box which is displayed, click on **New**. Enter your signature name in the New dialog box (see Figure 5.6). Click on the **Next** button. Enter your signature in this dialog box (see Figure 5.7), then click on **Finish**.

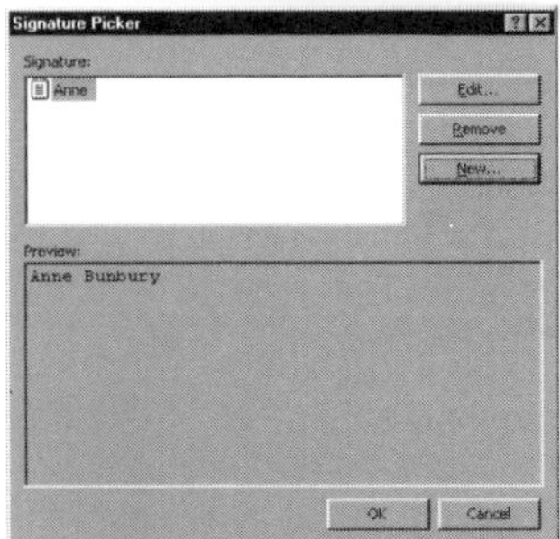

Figure 5.6: Creating a customised signature for your messages

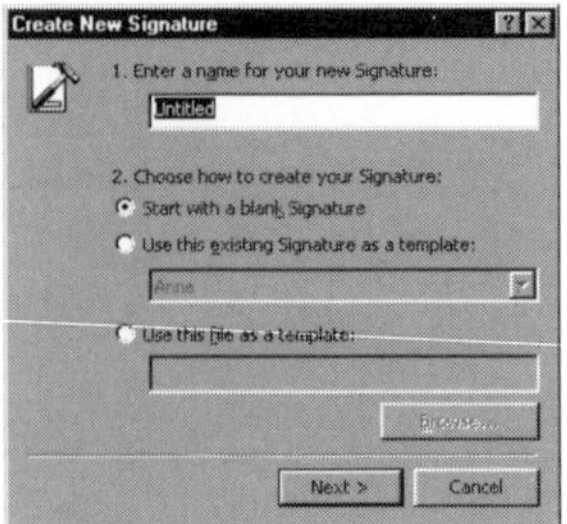

Figure 5.7: Entering your signature

Spell-checking

Outlook provides you with a spell-checker. To run it:

1. When you have finished your message, click on **Tools**, then select **Spelling** (see Figure 5.8).

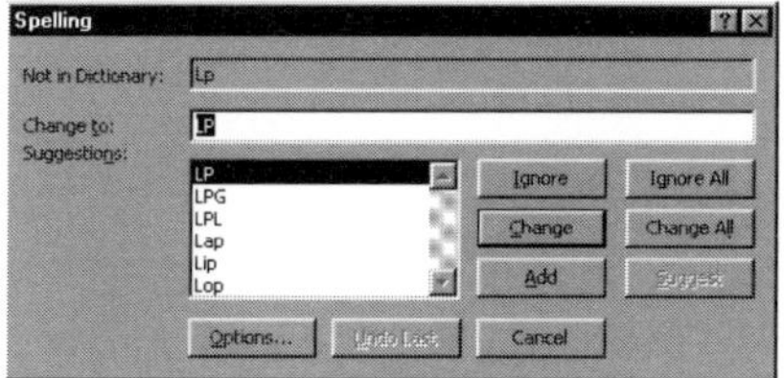

Figure 5.8: The spell-checker dialog box

2. Outlook displays the first misspelled word it finds in the **Not in Dictionary** field. You have the following options:

   – **Ignore.** The spell-checker does not change the word.

   – **Ignore All.** The spell-checker does not change any occurrence of this word throughout the text.

   – **Add.** Adds the word in question to the dictionary so that future occurrences will not be questioned.

   – **Change.** After selecting a suggested spelling from the **Suggestions** field, click on this button to change this occurrence of the word in question to the suggested spelling.

   – **Cancel.** Exits without completing the spell-check.

3. When the spell-check is complete, click on **OK** in the dialog box.

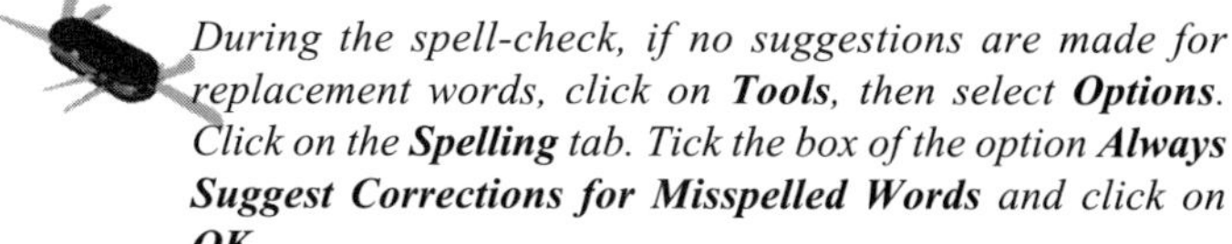

*During the spell-check, if no suggestions are made for replacement words, click on **Tools**, then select **Options**. Click on the **Spelling** tab. Tick the box of the option **Always Suggest Corrections for Misspelled Words** and click on **OK**.*

Formatting the text of messages

Outlook allows you to format the text in your messages by selecting the font style and size, colours, etc. to be used (see Figure 5.9). This formatting can be performed before or after text entry in the message box.

*If you do not select the option Formatted Text in the configuration of your messages (**Tools**, **Options**, **Text Format**), the toolbar will appear 'greyed' and you cannot use its formatting buttons.*

There are two possibilities for formatting:

- **Before text entry.** Click on the format of your choice or select the font style and size by clicking on the arrow in the drop-down lists and enter your text.
- **After text entry.** Select the word, phrase or text to be formatted, then click on the format of your choice or select the font style and size by clicking on the arrow in the drop-down lists.

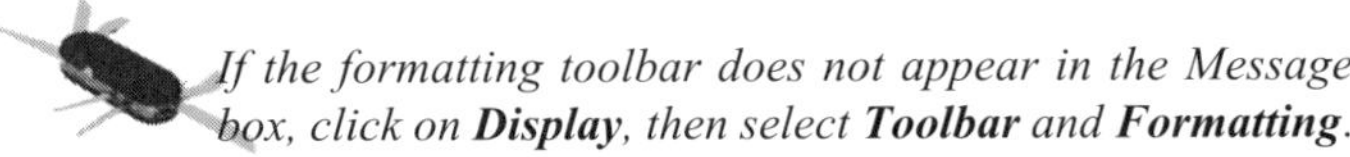

*If the formatting toolbar does not appear in the Message box, click on **Display**, then select **Toolbar** and **Formatting**.*

Figure 5.9: The formatting toolbar

Moving, copying, changing views, printing a message

All these procedures are identical to those for received messages. See Hour 4 for a reminder of them.

Displaying all sent messages

Outlook allows you to view all the messages you have sent.

To display them:

1. Click on **My Shortcuts**.
2. Click on **Sent Items** (see Figure 5.10).

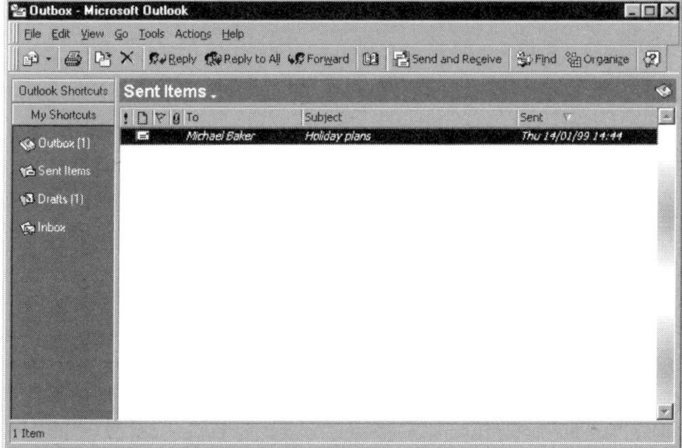

Figure 5.10: The Sent Items folder

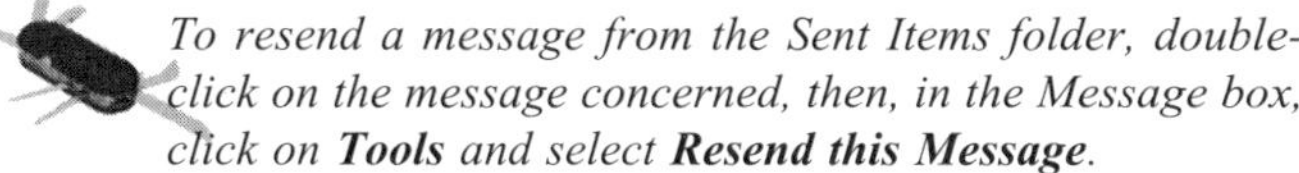

*To resend a message from the Sent Items folder, double-click on the message concerned, then, in the Message box, click on **Tools** and select **Resend this Message**.*

Deleting a message

To do this, use the Delete button (represented by an X) located in the Inbox or Message Box toolbars.

To delete a message:

1. In the Inbox, place the pointer on the message and click on it to select it.
2. Click on **Delete** in the toolbar.

*To delete several messages, click on the first message to be deleted, then press **Ctrl** and hold the key down. Then click on the second message to be deleted. When you have finished selecting the messages, click on **Delete** in the toolbar.*

THE DELETED ITEMS FOLDER

If you accidentally delete a message you wanted to keep, Outlook allows you to recover the item from a folder called Deleted Items. By default, everything you delete is placed in this folder.

To recover a deleted message:

1. Click on **Outlook Shortcuts** in the My Shortcuts bar.
2. Click on **Deleted Items** in the Outlook Shortcuts bar (see Figure 5.11).

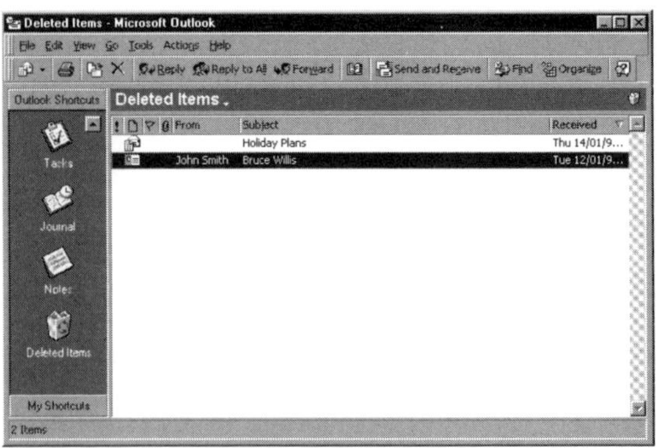

Figure 5.11: The Deleted Items folder

3. Click on the button opposite the message to be restored and hold the mouse button down.
4. Drag to the Inbox and release.

Your message is displayed once more in the Inbox folder.

The Deleted Items folder is like a wastepaper basket: as long as you haven't emptied it, it will still contain all the deleted items.

To empty the Deleted Items folder:

1. Click on **Deleted Items** in the Outlook Shortcuts bar.
2. Click on the message to be deleted, then on **Delete** in the toolbar.
3. A dialog box asks you to confirm this deletion; click on **Yes**.
4. Repeat this procedure for each of the elements to be deleted.

You can customise this option by deciding to empty this folder each time you exit Outlook. Click on ***Tools****, then select* ***Options****. Click on the* ***General*** *tab: in the* ***General Settings*** *area, tick the box of the option* ***Empty the Deleted Items Folder Upon Exiting*** *and click on* ***OK****.*

MANAGING AND CONFIGURING OUTGOING MESSAGES

Let us now look at configuring and managing your messages.

Configuring a message

As you saw at the beginning of this chapter, Outlook has a number of options for customising your messages (see Table 5.1). To edit these options, simply click on the **Options** button, then tick the box of the desired option or select a choice from the option drop-down list, so that Outlook will implement your options when sending the message. The options chosen will only be activated for the message for which you have specified them.

Two of these options (**Do Not Send Before,** and **Expires After**) open a calendar:

1. Click on the arrow of one of these options (see Figure 5.12).

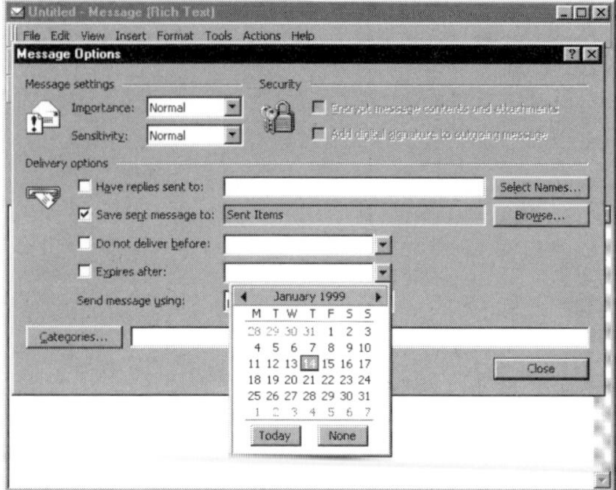

Figure 5.12: The drop-down list displays a calendar

2. Click on the date of your choice.

Other options offer choices which are opened by clicking on the arrow of the drop-down list (see Table 5.2).

Table 5.2: The choices in the Message Options box.

Option	Choice
Importance	High, Low or Normal
Sensitivity	Normal, Personal, Private or Confidential
Select names from the Have Replies Sent To field	Opens the list of address books and allows you to select a name
Browse the Save the Sent Message To field	Opens a list of folders from which you select a folder to which to copy the messages you send

Managing messages

You will soon be sending and receiving a lot of messages. In the Mail group, Outlook provides folders to help you organise them:

- **Notes Folder.** For drafting your messages before sending them.
- **Sent Items folder.** For keeping all messages already sent.
- **Outbox folder.** For all messages waiting to be sent.

If you wish to insert items into your messages, this procedure is identical to that already explained during Hour 3. Refer to that chapter for a reminder.

Table 5.3: Keyboard shortcuts for Hour 5.

Action	Keyboard shortcut
In the Inbox	
New message	**Ctrl-N**
In the Message box	
Open the Address Book	**Ctrl-Shift-B**
Choose an indicator	**Ctrl-W**
Send a message	**Enter**
Save a message	**Ctrl-S**
Check spelling	**F7**
In the Inbox or the Message box	
Delete a message	**Ctrl-D**

Table 5.4: Inbox folder symbols (in addition to those already mentioned in Hour 4).

Symbol	Description
	Message which has received a reply
	Message saved or not sent
	Notification that message has been read
	Attempted message reminder
	Notification of successful message reminder
	Notification of failed message reminder
	Notification that message has not been delivered
	Notification that message has not been read

Hour 6

The Calendar

The contents for this hour

- Calendar folder
- The Schedule
- Appointments, meetings and events
- The TaskPad
- Views

Calendar folder

This folder is used like a diary. It allows you to manage your time, to plan appointments, meetings and events in your professional or private life, to prepare lists of tasks and to make notes of important points.

To open the Calendar folder, click on the **Calendar** icon in the Outlook Shortcuts bar.

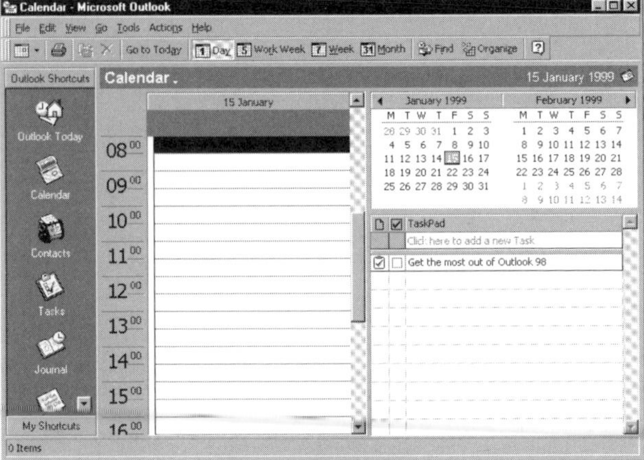

Figure 6.1: The Calendar folder screen

Basic items

The Calendar folder has three components:

- **Schedule pane.** A daily, weekly or monthly schedule in which you note all the important items in your activities, such as appointments, meetings and events.
- **Calendar pane.** A calendar which allows you to quickly navigate from one month to another, to view a specific day in the schedule.
- **TaskPad.** A list of tasks to be carried out. This item is directly linked to the Tasks folder.

The Calendar standard toolbar

In addition to the buttons common to all the toolbars, Table 6.1 lists the buttons specific to the Calendar toolbar.

Table 6.1: The buttons specific to the Calendar toolbar.

Button	Description
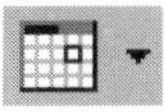	Dialog box for creating an appointment
 Go to Today	Goes to the current date (as set by the system clock)
 1 Day	Goes to the current day in the Schedule pane
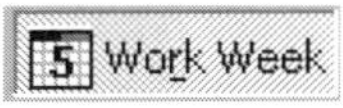 5 Work Week	Schedule for the next five days' work
 7 Week	Weekly schedule
 31 Month	Monthly schedule

Figure 6.2: The toolbar of the Calendar folder

Clicking on a toolbar button activates its function.

Calendar pane

The Calendar pane is a practical tool for rapidly accessing or changing a date (see Figure 6.3).

Figure 6.3: The Calendar pane

The current date is shadowed and framed in red. If you choose another date, the current date remains framed in red and the selected day appears shadowed. Each time you click on a date in the Calendar pane, it is displayed in the Schedule pane.

To navigate in the Calendar pane:

- a click on the left arrow of the Calendar pane displays the previous month;
- a click on the right arrow of the Calendar pane displays the following month;
- a click on the name of the month opens a list of all the possible months; select the month to access it;
- a click on a date in the Calendar pane displays the current day in the Schedule pane; and
- a click on a week number displays the selected week in the Schedule pane.

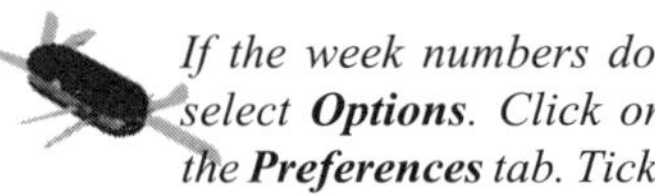

If the week numbers do not appear, click on ***Tools****, then select* ***Options****. Click on the* ***Calendar Options*** *button in the* ***Preferences*** *tab. Tick the box of the option* ***Display Week Numbers in the Calendar Pane;*** *click on* ***OK****.*

The Schedule

The Schedule is used for indicating your appointments, meetings and events.

Customising the Schedule

By default, the Schedule is daily with an hourly range of 8 am to 5 pm, and an hourly breakdown unit of 30 minutes (see Figure 6.4). To scroll through the hours, click on the scroll bar arrow.

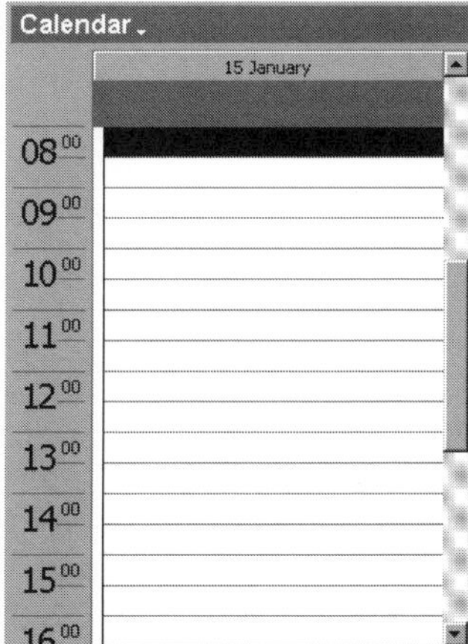

Figure 6.4: The Schedule displays the current day in intervals of 30 minutes

It may be necessary to change certain default parameters of your Schedule to make your work easier. For example, perhaps you never work on Wednesdays, or you arrive in the office at 9.30 in the morning. Outlook has a dialog box which allows you to configure all these parameters (see Figure 6.5). There is a good reason for this: you work as part of a network, which means that your colleagues should be able to invite you to meetings, make appointments for you, know your holiday dates, etc. To do this, they will consult your Schedule to find out when you are available.

To customise the Schedule:

1. Click on **Tools**, then select **Options**.
2. Click on the **Calendar Options** button.
3. Make the desired selections (working days, first working day, etc.).
4. When you have finished, click on **OK**.

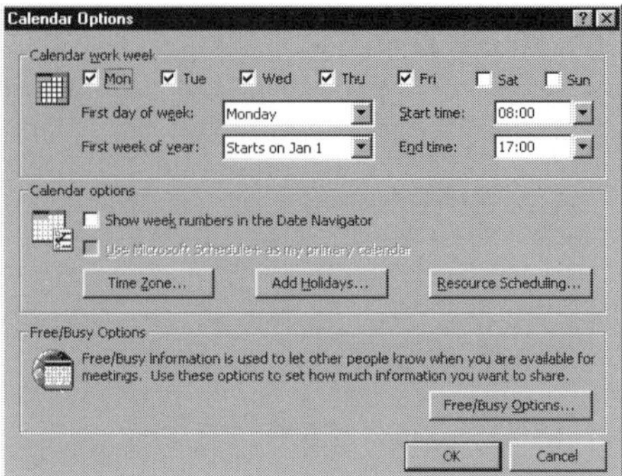

Figure 6.5: The box for customising the Schedule offers many options

Table 6.2: The customising options available.

Option	Description
Working week in the Calendar	A click in the box of one of the proposed days deletes this day in all the weeks of the Schedule
First day of the week	A click on the arrow of the drop-down list allows you to select the first working day of your week
First week of the year	A click on the arrow of the drop-down list allows you to select the first working week of the year
Working hours in the Calendar	A click on the arrow in the start field or end field allows you to specify your working timetable

The Availability Options button allows you to configure the options for the distribution of your Schedule on your company Intranet (see Hour 8).

APPOINTMENTS, MEETINGS AND EVENTS

Before continuing, it is important to understand the concept of these three activities:

- **Appointments.** This is an activity for which you allocate time in your Calendar; it therefore has an effect on your use of time.
- **Meeting.** This is an activity for which you allocate time in your Calendar, with an effect on your use of time and on that of others. In Hour 9, you will see how you can set up and schedule a meeting and invite other people to it.
- **Event.** This is an activity which lasts a minimum of 24 hours, such as a seminar or an exhibition. It may also be an event which occurs every year, such as a birthday or a trade show. However, this activity has no effect on your use of time.

Creating an appointment

To create an appointment, we shall use an actual example: you have an appointment at 10 am on 9 April 1999 with Mr Smith; this appointment should take about one hour.

To quickly create an appointment:

1. If necessary, display the month of April in the Calendar pane by clicking on the arrow to scroll through the months. When the month of April is displayed, click on **9**.
2. In the Schedule pane where the date of 9 April has just been displayed, click on the desired time slot, in this case **10 am**.
3. Enter a description of your appointment, then press **Enter**.
4. To specify the end of the appointment, i.e. 11 am, place the pointer in the lower part of the blue frame around the appointment, then click and drag to 11 am and release (see Figure 6.6).

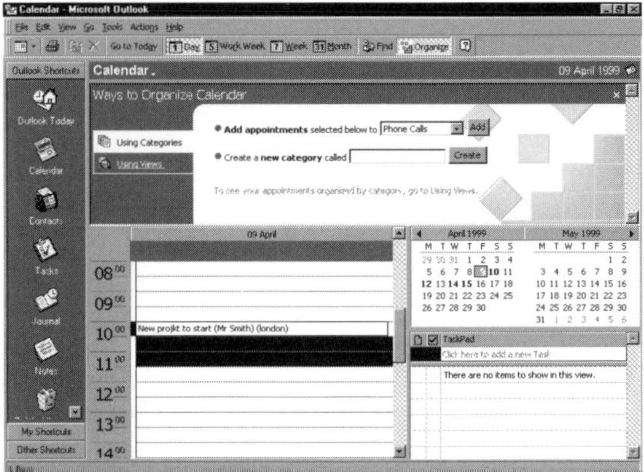

Figure 6.6: The appointment you have just created is displayed in the Schedule

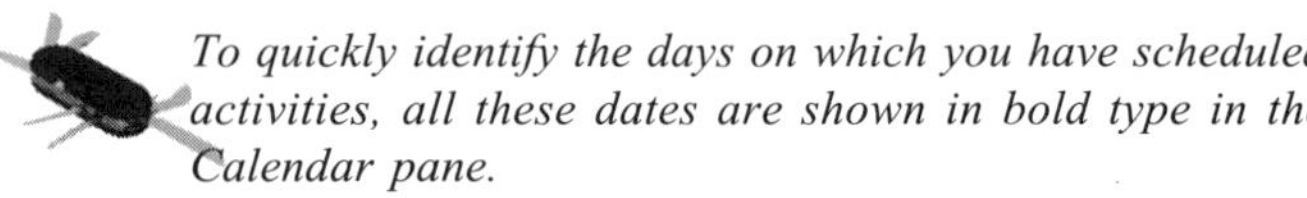

To quickly identify the days on which you have scheduled activities, all these dates are shown in bold type in the Calendar pane.

Now let's repeat the above example, but adding some of the options offered by Outlook (such as a beep to remind you of an appointment, the nature of the appointment, etc.).

You will use the New Appointment button in the Calendar toolbar. It is located at the extreme left of the toolbar.

To create a more detailed appointment:

1. Click on **New Appointment** in the toolbar.

   The Appointment box is displayed (see Figure 6.7).

2. If necessary, click on the **Appointment** tab and enter the name of the person you are meeting, the reason for the appointment, etc.

3. If you want, enter the location of the appointment.

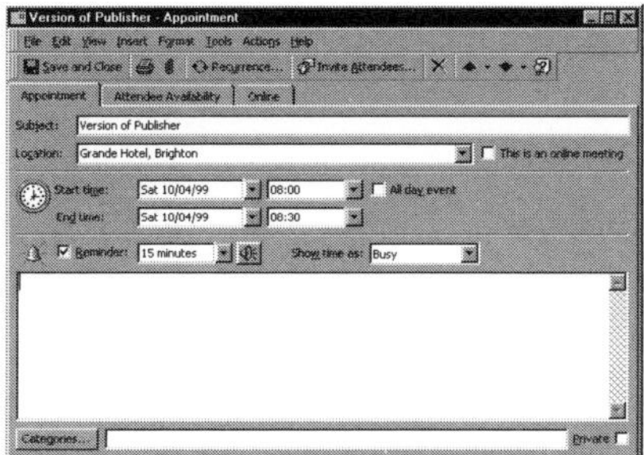

Figure 6.7: The Appointment box contains the options to be defined

4. Click on the arrow in the first text field of the **Start** option and select the desired date (see Figure 6.8), then click on the arrow in the second text field of the **Start** option and select the start time.

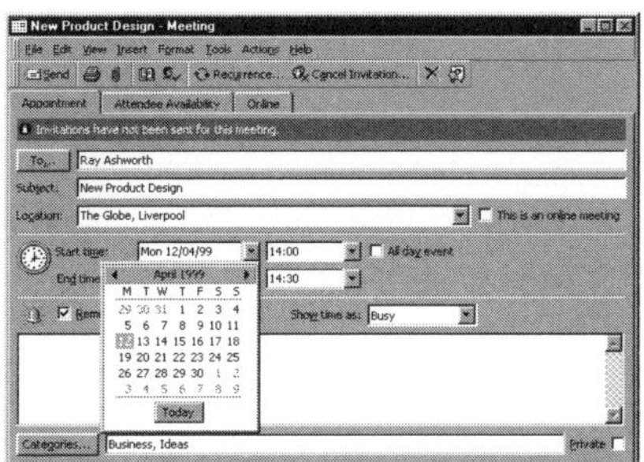

Figure 6.8: The first entry for the Start option opens a calendar

5. If you want, click on the arrow in the second text field of the **End** option and select the end time or tick the box of the **All day event** option.

6. If you want Outlook to beep before the appointment to remind you of it, tick the **Reminder** box, then click on the

arrow. Select the reminder period (by default, the reminder is triggered 15 minutes before the appointment).

7. So that the people who consult your Calendar will know your availability, click on the arrow of the **Show time as** option and select the option corresponding to your choice (**Free**, **Provisional**, **Busy, Out of the Office**).

8. If you wish, enter comments or notes concerning this appointment in the text field.

9. If you want to indicate the appointment category, click on **Categories** (see Figure 6.9), tick the box of the desired category, then click on **OK**.

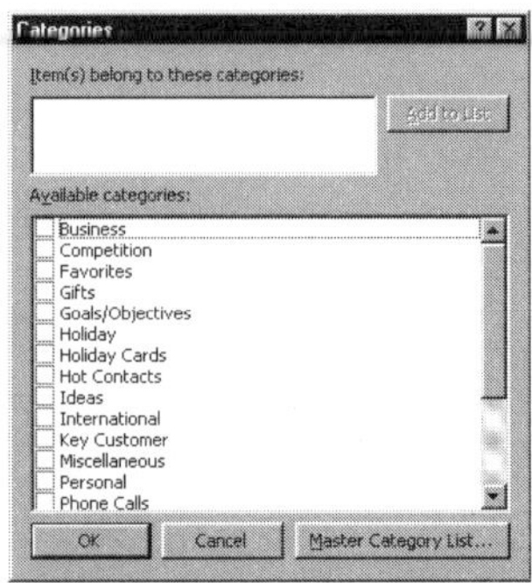

Figure 6.9: The Categories box

10. Finally, tick the **Private** option.

11. When you have finished, click on **Save and Close** in the toolbar.

The appointment is displayed in the Schedule for the day of your appointment (see Figure 6.10).

*To close the Appointment box without confirming any options, click on **File**, then select **Close**.*

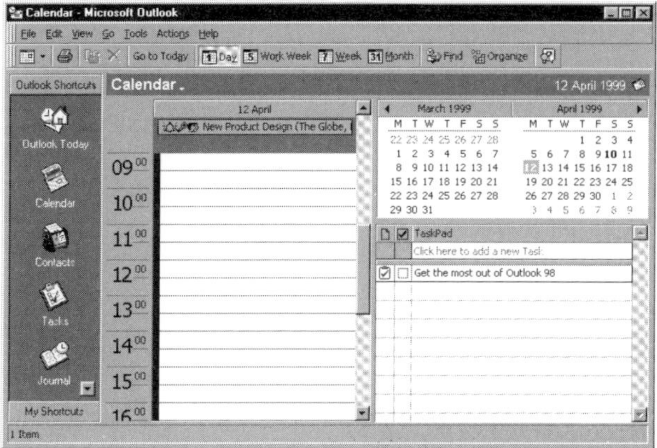

Figure 6.10: The appointment is displayed in your Schedule, showing the symbols corresponding to the options selected

Modifying an appointment

To make changes:

1. Display the day of the appointment by clicking on the date in the Calendar pane, then double-click on the appointment in the Schedule pane.

   The Appointment box is displayed.

2. Make your changes, then click on **Save and Close** in the toolbar.

*To delete an appointment, click on the appointment, then click on **Delete** in the toolbar.*

Creating a recurring appointment

Certain activities in your work are recurrent. For example, you might have a discussion with your manager every Friday.

Use the **Recurrence** button located in the toolbar of the Appointment window. It is represented by two arrows forming a circle.

To create a recurrent appointment:

1. Click on **New Appointment** in the toolbar.
2. If necessary, click on the **Appointment** tab, then enter the subject of the appointment.
3. Click on **Recurrence** in the toolbar.

   The Appointment Recurrence dialog box is displayed (see Figure 6.11).

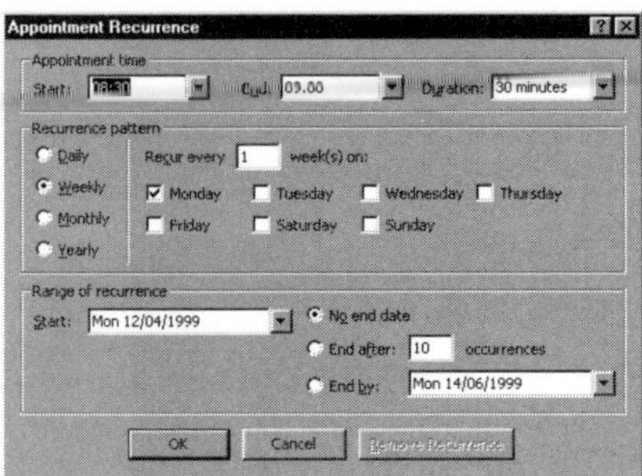

Figure 6.11: The Appointment Recurrence box

4. In the **Appointment time** zone, click on the arrow in the **Start** field and select the start time, then, if necessary, click on the arrow in the **Duration** field and select the desired duration (the **End** field will then be completed automatically).
5. In the **Recurrence pattern** zone, tick the box opposite the desired option, then tick the required day (for a weekly recurrence).
6. In the **Range of recurrence** zone, click on the arrow in the **Start** field and select the start date for this recurrent appointment.

7. Tick the desired option for the end date. You have a choice between: no end date, specifying the number of appointments necessary for this activity, or an end date set in advance.
8. Click on **OK**.
9. In the Appointment dialog box, select any other required options (Private, Reminder, Categories, Location, etc.).
10. Click on **Save and Close** in the toolbar.

Creating an event

As previously mentioned, an event is an activity which lasts at least 24 hours but that does not affect your Schedule.

To create an event:

1. Click on **Actions**, then select **New All Day Event**.

   The Event box appears (see Figure 6.12).

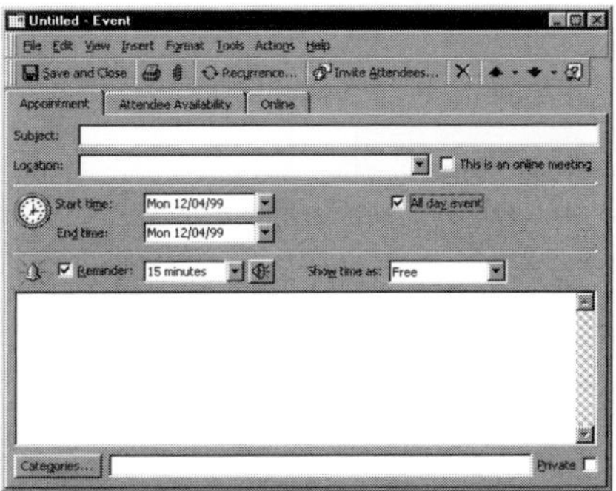

Figure 6.12: The Event box is displayed; it is very similar to the Appointment box

2. Enter the definition of the event in the **Subject** box.
3. Enter the location of the event in the **Location** box, if required.

4. Click on the arrow beside the **Start time** box and select the desired day, then click on the arrow beside the **End time** box and choose the end day.
5. Make sure the **All Day Event** box is ticked.
6. If you want to be reminded of this event, tick the **Reminder** box, then click on the arrow. Select the reminder period before the event if you want to change the default reminder period of 15 minutes.
7. If you want to, you can indicate your availability, make comments and select a category.
8. Click on **Save and Close** in the toolbar.

   The event is displayed at the head of the Schedule pane for the day concerned, in a greyed section (see Figure 6.13).

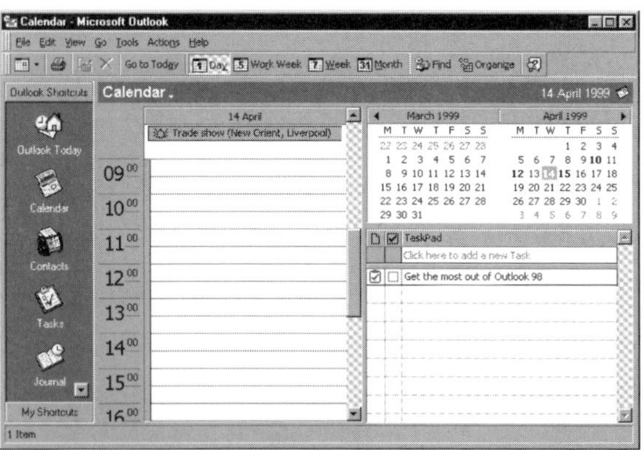

Figure 6.13: The event is displayed at the head of the Schedule for the day concerned

To modify an event:

1. Display the day of the event, then double-click on the event in the Schedule.
2. Make your changes, then click on **Save and Close** in the toolbar.

To delete an event:

1. Click on the event to be deleted.
2. Click on **Delete** in the toolbar.

*To create a recurring event, click on **Actions**, then select **New All Day Event**. In the box, click on **Recurrence**, make your choice and click on **OK** when you have finished. In the Event dialog box, enter the required options, then click on **Save and Close** in the toolbar.*

Creating a meeting

The procedure for creating a meeting is the same as for creating an appointment except that you organise the meeting using advanced scheduling. In Hour 9, you will see how to create and organise a meeting.

The other Schedule options

Outlook also allows you to display your holidays, as follows:

1. Click on the first day of your holidays in the Calendar pane.
2. Click on **Actions**, then select **New All Day Event**.
3. In the **Subject** field, Enter **Holidays**.
4. In the **End time** field, click on the arrow and select the date of return from holidays.
5. Click on **Save and Close** in the toolbar.

   Your holidays will now appear as an event in your Schedule (see Figure 6.14).

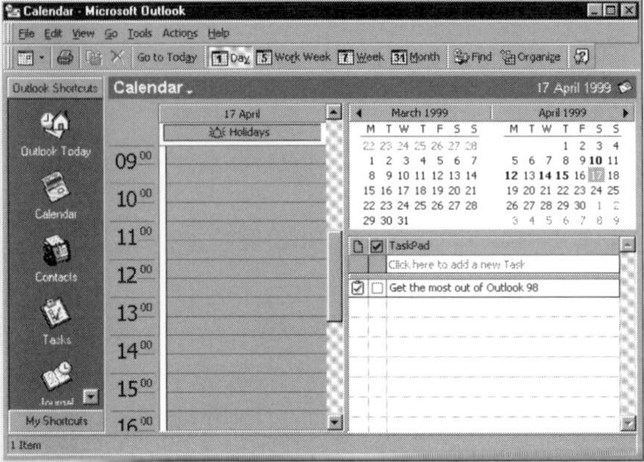

Figure 6.14: Your holidays displayed in your Schedule

Outlook can display public holidays for the country in which you are working or those of another country:

1. Click on **Tools**, then select **Options**.
2. Click on the **Calendar Options** button.
3. Click on **Add Holidays**.
3. Tick the box opposite the required country (see Figure 6.15).
4. Click on **OK**.

Figure 6.15: The Add Holidays to Calendar box

Finding an appointment

Use the **Find** button in the standard toolbar.

To find an item:

1. Click on **Find Items** in the toolbar (see Figure 6.16).

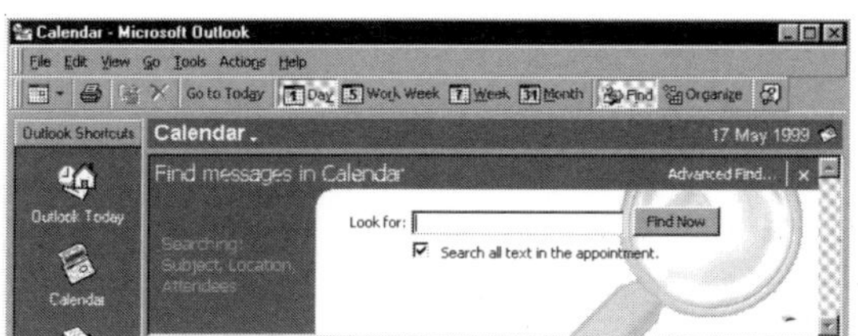

Figure 6.16: The Find Items pane

2. In the **Look for** field, enter an item of the appointment (the name of the person, the company, etc.), then click on **Find Now**.

   Outlook displays the result of the search in the form of a table (see Figure 6.17).

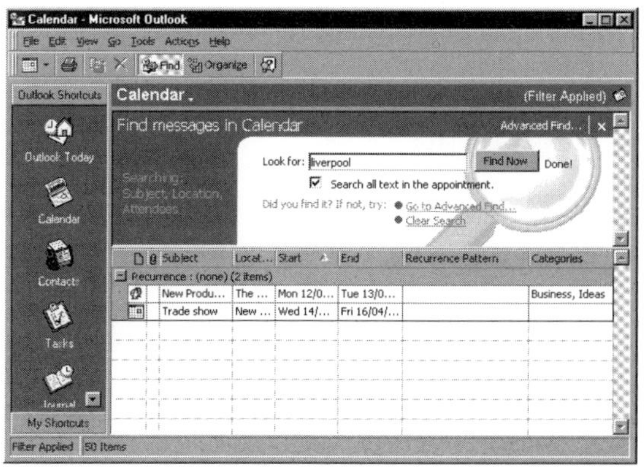

Figure 6.17: The result of the search shown as a table

3. Double-click on the button opposite the appointment displayed if you want to alter one or more elements.
4. Click on the **Close** button in the Appointment box.
5. Click on the **Close** button in the Find Items pane.

The TaskPad

This corresponds to the Tasks folder. To create, modify, schedule or move a task, see Hour 7.

Views

Outlook offers several different ways of viewing your calendar.

To modify the view of your calendar, click on **View, Current View**. In the drop-down menu which is displayed, select the type of view you want. The Define Calendar Views command allows you to customise the views.

The Day/Week/Month view is active by default. To modify this default view, click on the **Organise** button. In the pane which is displayed, click on the option **Using Views**. Select the default view mode you want. Close the view pane.

You can also display a more detailed view of an appointment without opening the corresponding appointment record. To do this, in the day concerned, click on the relevant appointment to select it. Click on **View, Preview Pane**. A detailed description of the appointment is displayed in the lower part of the Schedule pane. To return to the default view mode, click on **Display, Preview Pane**.

Table 6.3: Keyboard shortcuts for Hour 6.

Action	Keyboard shortcut
New appointment (after selection)	**Ctrl-N**
Delete an appointment (after selection)	**Del**
Open the Appointment box (after selection)	**Ctrl-Shift-A**
Go to a date	**Ctrl-G**
Close the Appointment box	**Alt-G**

Table 6.4: Calendar folder symbols.

Button	Description
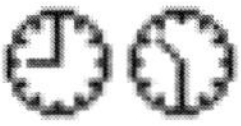	Start and End times
	Recurrent appointment or meeting
	Calendar item with an attachment
	Private appointment or meeting
	Beep reminder before appointment or meeting

Hour 7

Tasks

THE CONTENTS FOR THIS HOUR

- Tasks folder
- Creating a task
- Views
- Managing tasks

TASKS FOLDER

In Outlook 98, a task is a work-related or personal job which you follow through to completion. It may be completed in one or more sessions (these are called recurrent tasks).

The Tasks folder corresponds to the schedule for your different jobs. You sort your tasks by order of importance and monitor their progress. You can also assign tasks to your colleagues and receive progress reports on the various jobs. You will see how to allocate tasks in Hour 9.

To open the Tasks folder, click on the **Tasks** icon in the Outlook Shortcuts bar.

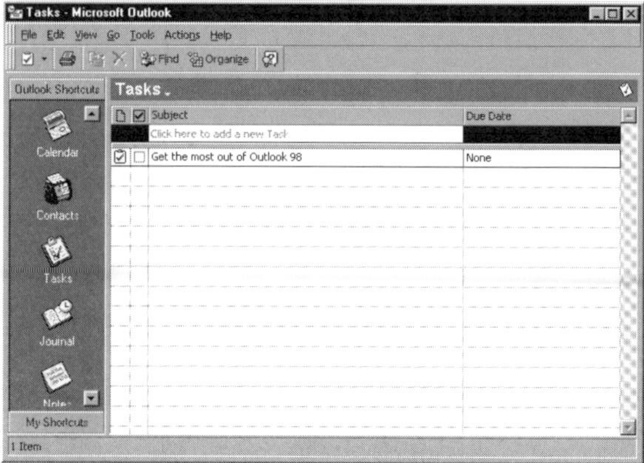

Figure 7.1: The screen of the Tasks folder

Standard toolbar of the Tasks folder

In addition to the icons common to all toolbars, Table 7.1 lists the icons specific to the Tasks toolbar.

Table 7.1: Icons specific to the Tasks toolbar.

Icon	Description
	Opens a dialog box to create a task
Find	Allows you to quickly find a task
Organize	Allows you to organise the Tasks folder

Clicking on an icon in the toolbar activates its function.

Tasks folder indicators

These are accessible in the task list window, and allow you to display the options for each task. Some allow you to choose an option directly from the table (such as the importance, progress, due date, % completion and categories of task). These indicators are displayed and available according to the view selected. Outlook differentiates tasks by those in progress, late tasks and completed tasks.

Tasks are assigned as one of the following:

- **Active Tasks.** (in ordinary characters).
- **Completed Tasks.** (in greyed strikeout characters).
- **Overdue Tasks.** (in red characters).

Table 7.2: Tasks folder indicators

Views	Indicator	Description
All, except the Timeline view		The task type (periodical, normal, etc.)
Simple List		The task status (completed or not)
All, except Simple List and Timeline view		The importance of the task (major, minor, etc.)
All, except Simple List and Timeline view		The presence of attachments in the task is displayed
All, except the Timeline view	Subject	Description of the task

Table 7.2: Tasks folder indicators (cont.).

Views	Indicator	Description
All, except the Timeline view	Due date	The deadline for completion of the task
Detailed List, Active Tasks, Next Seven Days, Assignment and By Person Responsible	Status	The status of the task (completed or not)
Completed Tasks	Completed on	The due date you have indicated for the task
Completed Tasks, Next Seven Days, Active Tasks and Detailed List	Categories	The task category
Detailed List, Active Tasks and Next Seven Days	% completed	The task progress percentage
Assignment and By Person Responsible	Owner	The owner of the task, i.e. the name of the person who created the task (necessary for the task assignment option)
By Person Responsible	Requested by	The name of the person who has requested completion of this task (necessary for the task assignment option)

Later in this chapter, you will see learn how to use these indicators to group, sort and enter them directly in the list of tasks.

Creating a task

You will now learn how to create a task.

Toolbar of the task creation box

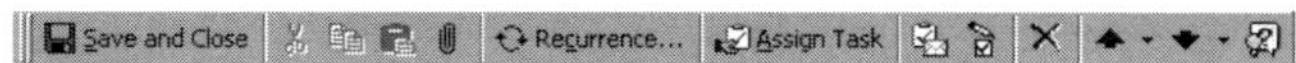

Figure 7.2: The toolbar of the task creation box

Clicking on an icon in the toolbar activates it.

Creating a task

If you want to produce a report, prepare for a meeting, etc., which you will only do once, click on **New Task** in the toolbar in the Tasks folder. The task creation box opens (see Figure 7.3).

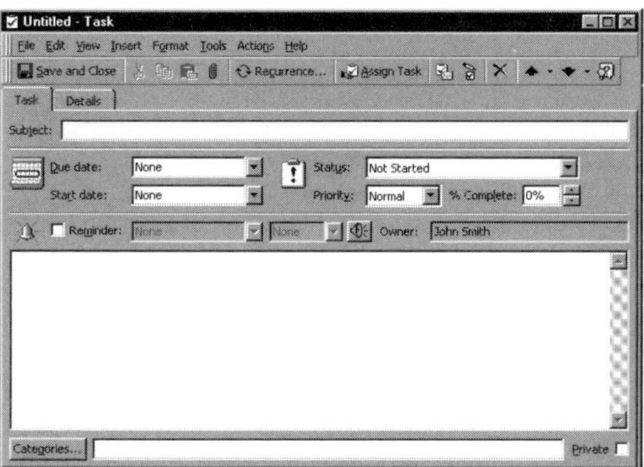

Figure 7.3: The box for creating tasks

Click on the **Task** tab. In the **Subject** field, enter the subject of your task. In the **Due date** field, click on the arrow, then choose **None** if you do not want to specify a date for the end of your task, or select the scheduled due date from the drop-down calendar. To indicate the start date for the task, click on the arrow in the **Start date** option (a drop-down calendar opens), and click on the date desired for the start of your task (see Figure 7.4).

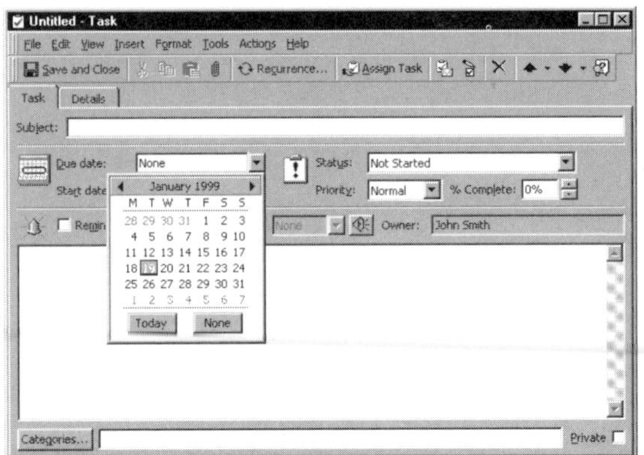

Figure 7.4: The Due date and Start date options open a calendar

If you want to indicate a status for your task, click on the arrow in the **Status** option and select your choice (see Table 7.3). If you want to indicate a priority level, click on the arrow in the **Priority** option and select your choice (see Table 7.3). If you want to indicate the progress of the task, click on the arrow in the **% Complete** option, then select the desired percentage. If you want Outlook to beep to remind you of your task, click in the **Reminder** box, then click on the arrow in the **Reminder** option (a calendar opens). Click on the date desired for your reminder, then click on the arrow in the option showing a loudspeaker and select the required time for the reminder. If you want to indicate a category for your task, click on **Categories** (see Figure 7.5).

When you have indicated a due date for your task, a message appears in the Task box, indicating the number of days remaining before the due date.

Figure 7.5: The Categories box is displayed. Choose the relevant category

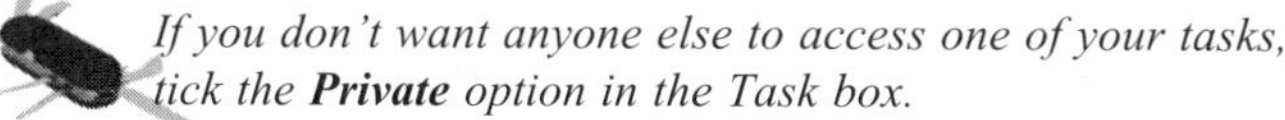

If you don't want anyone else to access one of your tasks, tick the ***Private*** *option in the Task box.*

Tick the box of the desired category. Click on **OK**. When you have finished, click on **Save and Close**.

The task you have just created is displayed in the Tasks folder table (see Figure 7.6).

To delete a task, click on the desired task in the task list and click on ***Delete*** *in the toolbar.*

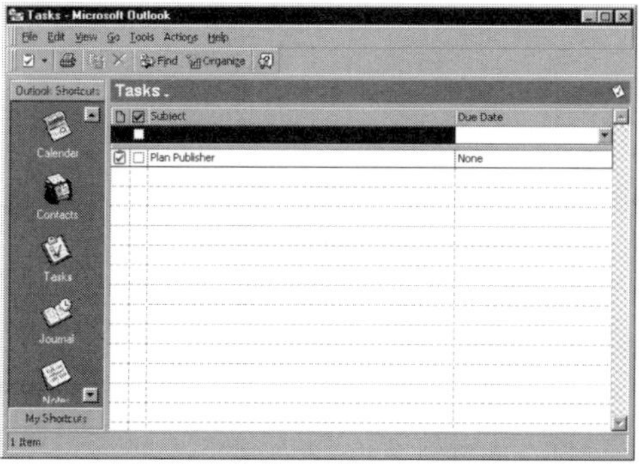

Figure 7.6: Your task is displayed in the Tasks folder

When you choose to indicate a due date for your task, by default the due date is the current date and the start date field remains empty: don't forget to indicate the start date.

Table 7.3: The various choices available with certain Task box options.

Option	Choices available
Status	Not started, In progress, Completed, Waiting on someone else, Deferred
Priority	Normal, Low, High
% Complete	25%, 50%, 75%, 100%

In the Task box, you are the default owner of the task. To transfer ownership to another person, see the section "Assigning Tasks" in Hour 9.

Creating a recurrent task

A recurrent task is:

- a job which is repeated at regular intervals, such as calculation of salaries, or
- a job which is renewed after its due date; for example, when monitoring of expense notes for January is finished, monitoring of expense notes for February begins.

To create a recurrent task:

1. In the Tasks folder, click on **New Task** in the toolbar.
2. Click on the **Task** tab.
3. In the **Subject** field, enter the subject of your task.

4. Click on **Recurrence** in the toolbar.

   The Task Recurrence box is displayed (see Figure 7.7).

*To delete the recurrence of a task, double-click on the task. In the Task box, click on **Recurrence** in the toolbar, then on **Remove Recurrence**, and finally on **OK** in the Task Recurrence box. In the Task box, click on **Save and Close**.*

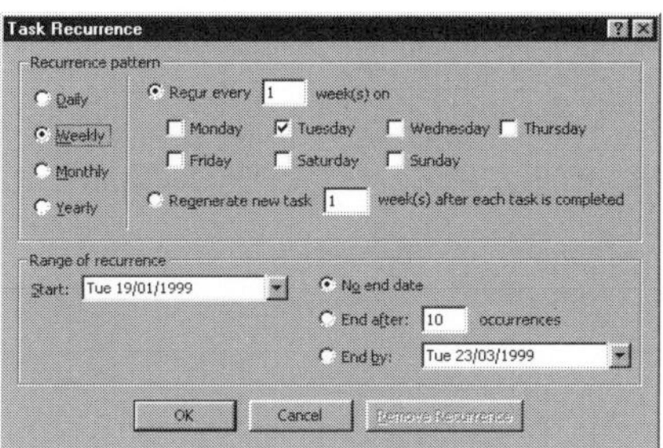

Figure 7.7: The Task Recurrence box

5. Tick the Recurrence desired.
6. Tick the options of your choice (days, weeks, etc.).
7. If necessary, tick the option **Regenerate new task**.
8. In the **Range of recurrence** field, click on the arrow in the **Start** option and select the date desired.
9. Tick the **No end date** option if you do not wish to indicate an end date. Or tick the **End after** option, then specify after how many occurrences you wish your task to end. Or tick in the **End by** option, then click on the arrow and select an end date from the Calendar which opens.
10. Click on **OK**.

    Returning to the Task box, repeat the procedure from step 7.

To modify a task, double-click on it in your list of tasks and make your changes. When you have finished, click on ***Save and Close*** *in the toolbar.*

More information on the completion of a task

Outlook offers the option of managing the monitoring and status of the task, its progress, the number of hours spent on completing it and its cost.

Before entering the time options, it is essential to specify to Outlook how many hours a day you actually work.

To monitor your task:

1. In the Tasks folder, double-click on the task concerned or click on **New Task** in the toolbar.
2. In the Task box, click on the **Details** tab (see Figure 7.8).
3. Enter the options desired (see Table 7.4).
4. When you have finished, click on **Save and Close** in the toolbar.

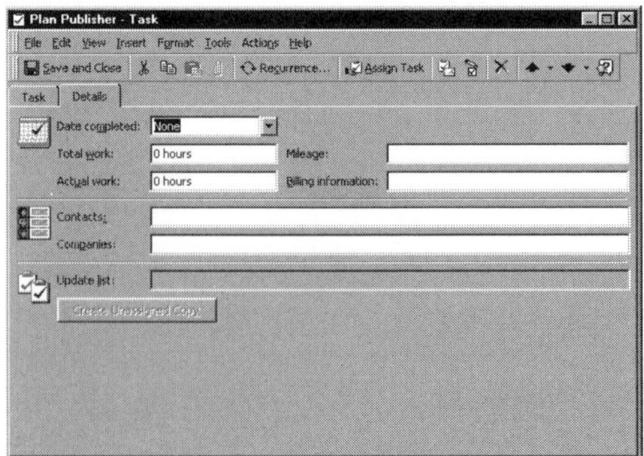

Figure 7.8: The Details tab in the Task box

Table 7.4: Details tab options

Option	Records
Date completed	The date on which the task is completed. Click on the arrow in the option and select the date you wish in the calendar which appears.
Total work	The estimated time for completion of the task. Click on the text field and enter the estimated number of hours.
Actual work	The time it actually took to complete the task. Click on the text field and enter the number of actual hours.
Mileage	The number of miles travelled to complete the task. Click on the text field and enter the figure.
Billing information	The total amount of expenses incurred in completing the task. Click on the text field and enter the amount.
Companies	The names of companies associated with the task. Click on the text field and enter the relevant names.
Contacts	The names of contacts associated with the task. Click on the text field and enter the relevant names.

Recording all this information allows you to prepare statistics on the completion of tasks. You will be able to assess time and costs in order to improve your task management. It is an effective way to monitor progress of a job.

*In the **Total work** and **Actual work** fields, the number of hours entered is converted into a number of days depending on the number of hours per working day entered when customising the calendar. For example, if you work 6 hours a day and have entered 12 hours for completion of your task, Outlook records two days' work.*

VIEWS

Like the other Outlook folders, Tasks offers a number of views. Each view offers the indicators shown in Table 7.2.

The views are:

- **Simple List.** Displays a list of tasks with the subject, due date, status and task type as an icon.
- **Detailed List.** Displays a list of tasks with the task type as an icon, the importance of the task, the presence of attachments in the task, the subject, the status, the due date, the completion percentage and the category.
- **Active Tasks.** Displays a list of unfinished tasks with indicators identical to those for the Detailed List.
- **Next Seven Days.** Displays a list of tasks scheduled for the following week with the task type as an icon, the importance of the task, the presence of attachments, the subject, the status, the due date, the completion percentage and the category.
- **Overdue Tasks.** Displays a list of overdue tasks with the same indicators as for the Detailed List.
- **By category.** Displays a list of the categories with the same indicators as for the Detailed List. To open a category, click on the + button; the tasks contained in this category are displayed.
- **Assignment.** Displays a list of tasks which have been allocated to you with the task type as an icon, the importance of the task, the presence of attachments in the task, the subject, the owner, the due date and the status.

- **By Person Responsible.** Displays a list of tasks according to the people who have assigned them, with the task type as an icon, the importance of the task, the presence of attachments in the task, the subject, the name of the person who requested it, the owner of the task, the due date and the status.
- **Completed Tasks.** Displays a list of finished tasks with the task type as an icon, the importance of the task, the presence of attachments in the task, the subject, the due date, the end date and the category.
- **Task Timeline.** Displays a list of tasks for each day, week or month (see Figure 7.9).

To modify the view of your list of tasks, click on **View,** then **Current View**. Select the view you want from the drop-down menu.

By default, the Simple List view is selected. If you want to modify the default view, click on the **Organize** button in the standard toolbar. Click on the **Using Views** option. Select the view you want from the list. Close the view pane.

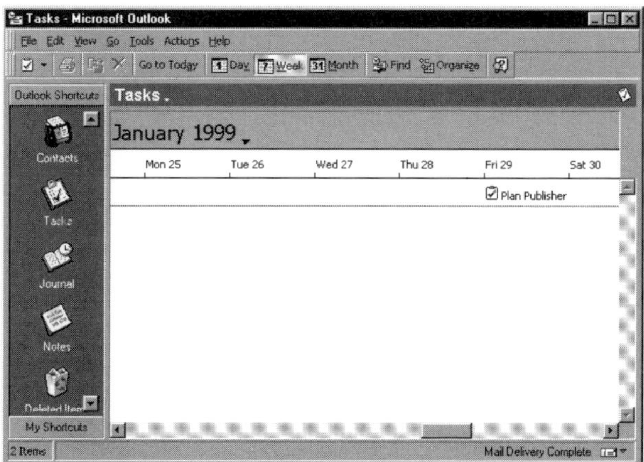

Figure 7.9: The timeline view of the Tasks folder

MANAGING TASKS

When you have created all your tasks, the list will appear in the Tasks folder. Using this list, you will be able to classify, sort, group, move and copy your list of tasks.

When there are several tasks in a list, besides viewing them in a folder, Outlook allows you to recall them by screens. For example, on starting the program, a message can remind you of the day's tasks (see Figure 7.10).

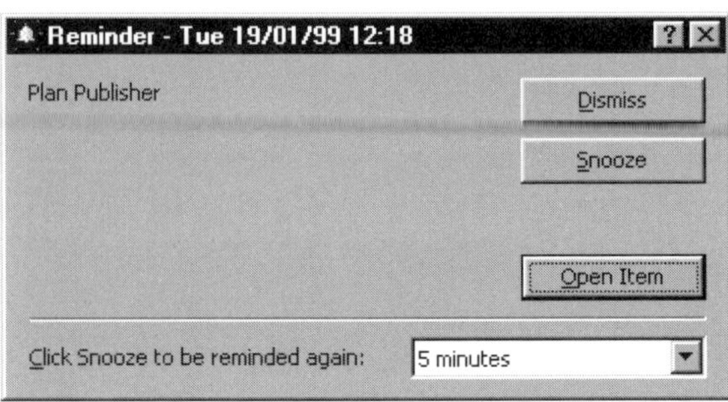

Figure 7.10: Outlook displays a reminder box for each of your day's tasks

You will not be reminded of a task if it does not have a due date.

To mark a task as completed:

1. Click on the box of the status indicator column (see Table 7.2).
2. A tick appears when the task is completed. It is greyed and struck through; you need only click on the ticked box to reactivate it.

To quickly add a task:

1. Click on the indicator indicating the task type (see Table 7.2).
2. In the greyed part displayed at the top of the list of tasks, click and enter a description of your task in the Subject indicator, then enter any other necessary information.

To move a task:

1. Click on the **Organize** button.
2. Click on the **Using Folders** option.
3. Select the folder to which you want to move the task.
4. Click on the **Move** button.

To group tasks, click on the indicator by which you want to group them (see Figure 7.11).

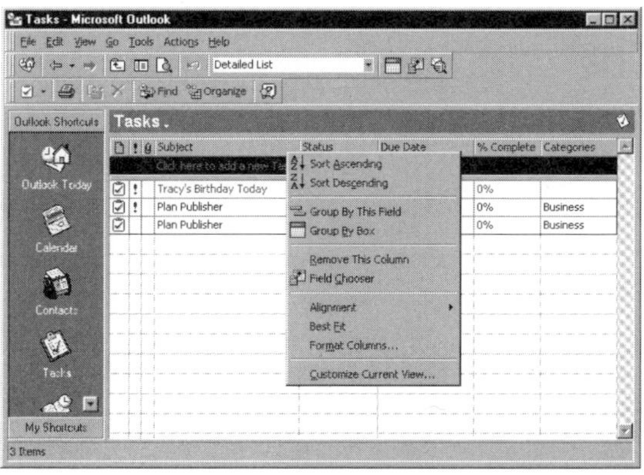

Figure 7.11: Using indicators to group tasks

To quickly find a task, click on the **Find** button in the standard toolbar (see Figure 7.12). Enter a keyword for the task to be found, then click on the **Find Now** button. The task found is displayed in a table. Double-click on its icon to view it.

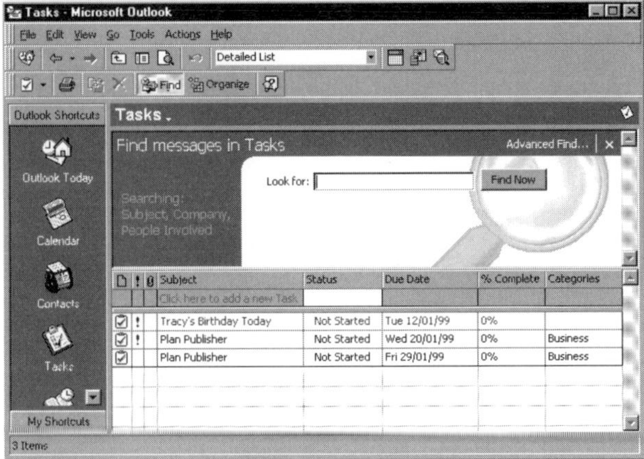

Figure 7.12: Quickly finding a task

Table 7.5: Keyboard shortcuts for Hour 7.

Action	Keyboard shortcut
In the Task box	
New task	**Ctrl-N**
Recurrence	**Ctrl-G**
Save	**Ctrl-S**
In the Tasks folder	
New task	**Ctrl-Shift-K**
Delete a task	**Ctrl-D**

Table 7.6: Task symbols.

Symbol	Description
	Task
	Completed task
	Task with attachment
	Task of minor importance
	Task of major importance
	Recurrent task

Hour 8

The Journal and Notes

The contents for this hour

- Journal folder
- Creating a Journal entry
- Journal views
- Notes folder
- Creating notes
- Managing and modifying notes
- Views

Journal folder

This folder acts as your "activity log". You can record meetings or conversations with your contacts, memorise information, messages and important files, and so on. You can also create Journal entries which have no connection to any specific item.

In addition to Outlook items, you can record items created in other Microsoft applications installed on your computer.

There are two types of automatic recording:

- **Automatic recording of Outlook items.** E-mail, replies to requests for meetings, task requests, replies to task requests.
- **Automatic recording of documents created in other programs.** Access, Excel, Office Binder, PowerPoint, Word and all other programs compatible with Microsoft Office.

To open the Journal folder, click on the **Journal** icon in the Outlook Shortcuts bar.

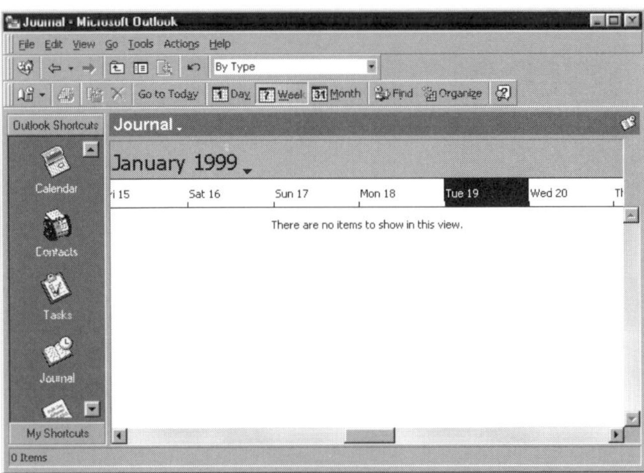

Figure 8.1: The Journal folder screen

Standard toolbar of the Journal folder

In addition to the icons common to all the toolbars, Table 8.1 list the icons specific to the Journal toolbar. To activate a function in the toolbar, simply click on its icon.

Table 8.1: The buttons specific to the Journal toolbar.

Button	Description
	Opens a dialog box to create a Journal entry
Go to Today	Allows you to go directly to the current day (according to the system clock)
1 Day	Allows you to view the entries for the selected day
7 Week	Allows you to view Journal entries for a specific week
31 Month	Allows you to view Journal entries for a specific month

Creating a Journal entry

To assist you in creating entries, the Journal Entry box has its own toolbar (see Figure 8.2).

Figure 8.2: The Journal Entry toolbar

Clicking on an icon in the toolbar activates its function.

Manually creating a Journal entry without a link to any item

You can create a Journal entry without any direct relationship to an Outlook item. For example, imagine you are canvassing and want to note the result of your phone call in the Journal. However, the customer in question is not in your list of contacts.

You can create an entry for the customer you have just phoned, as follows:

1. Click on **New Journal** in the toolbar.

   The Journal Entry box is displayed (see Figure 8.7).
2. In the **Subject** field, enter a description of your entry.
3. By default, Outlook displays Phone call in the **Entry type** field. Because there is no link to an item, accept this type.
4. In the **Company** field, enter the name of the company concerned.
5. In the **Start time** field, the current date appears. If you want to accept this date, click on the arrow to indicate the time.
6. If you want to, in the **Duration** field, click on the arrow and select the duration desired.
7. If you want to, click on **Categories**, tick the box of the category desired, then click on **OK**.
8. Enter any comments in the text field.
9. When you have finished, click on **Save and Close**.
10. In the Journal folder, click on the + button opposite the Call entry type, and your Journal entry will be displayed in the list (see Figure 8.3).

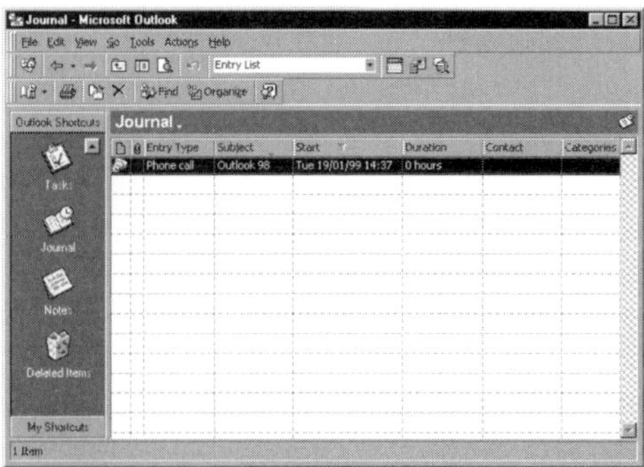

Figure 8.3: The Call entry screen

*To delete a Journal entry, click on the relevant entry in the list, then on **Delete** in the toolbar.*

*When you open the Journal Entry box, Outlook displays the current date and time in the **Start** field. You can change this date if you wish to.*

*To open an item from the Journal entry, double-click on the item shortcut in the text field of the Journal Entry box. To close the shortcut and return to the Journal Entry box, click on **File**, then select **Close**.*

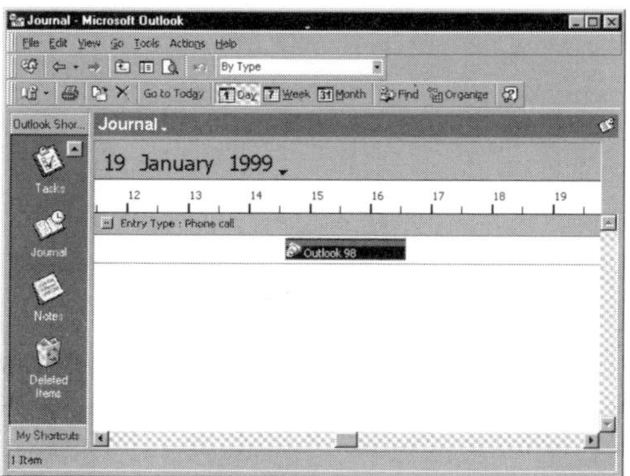

Figure 8.4: The entry type selected in the Journal Entry box displays the item you have just entered in the Journal

*To modify a Journal entry in the Journal folder, double-click on the entry in the list, make your changes, then click on **Save and Close**.*

Recording a phone call in the Journal

When you call one of your contacts, you may want to record the call in your Journal.

To record a phone call in the Journal, you must have a modem.

To create this entry:

1. In the Contacts Folder, click on the contact you want to call, then click on **Actions** and select **Call Contact**.
2. Click on the number to be dialled.

   The New Call box is displayed (see Figure 8.5).

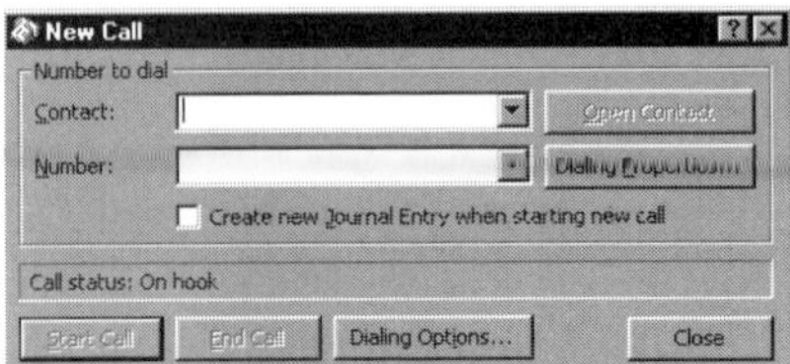

Figure 8.5: The New Call box

3. Tick **Create new Journal Entry when starting new call**.
4. Click on **Start Call**.
5. Pick up your telephone and click on **Speak**.

   The Journal Entry box is displayed together with the Call Status box (see Figure 8.6).

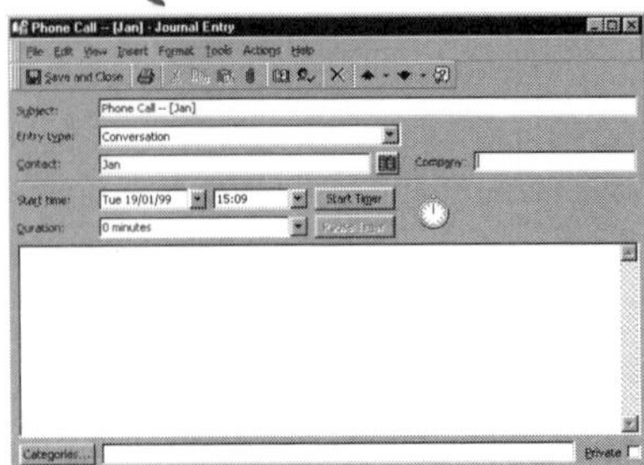

Figure 8.6: The Journal Entry box is displayed

6. Enter any notes concerning this discussion in the text field.
7. When the call is finished, click on **Pause Timer**.
8. Click on **Save and Close** in the toolbar.
9. In the New Call box, click on **End of Call**, then **Close**.

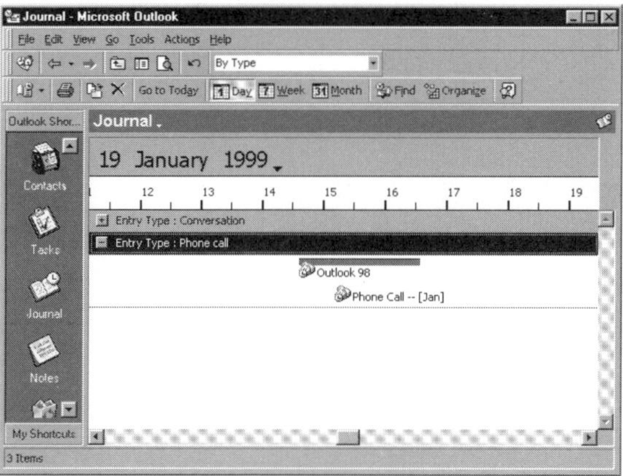

Figure 8.7: Your phone call is stored

Automatically creating an entry

This function allows you to automatically record items or statistics about Office documents which you have created in Outlook or in any other Microsoft application. To record automatically you need only configure Outlook and everything referring to your contact will be recorded in the Journal in the item associated with the contact (i.e. e-mail message, meeting request, etc.).

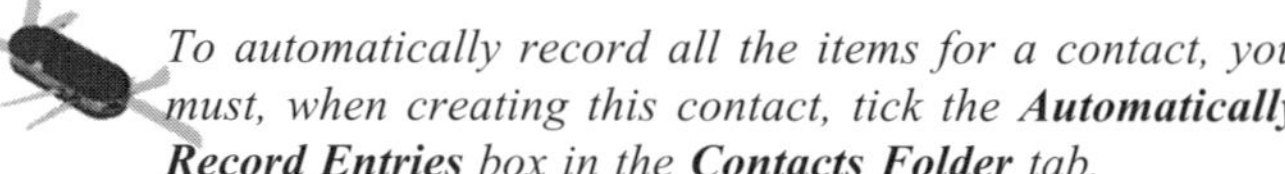

*To automatically record all the items for a contact, you must, when creating this contact, tick the **Automatically Record Entries** box in the **Contacts Folder** tab.*

To configure automatic recording:

1. In the Journal folder, click on **Tools**, then select **Options**.
2. In the **Preferences** tab, click on the **Journal Options** button (see Figure 8.8).

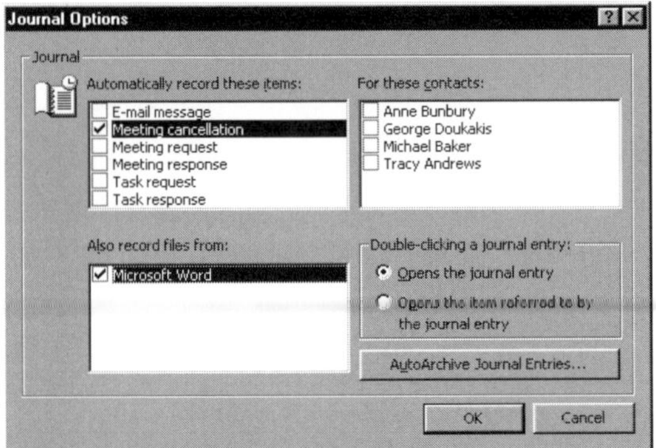

Figure 8.8: The options in the Journal Options box allow you to configure automatic recording

3. Tick the items you want to record in the Journal.
4. Click on the contacts for which you want to record these items.
5. If you want to record all the documents of an application in the Journal, tick the required application box.
6. Click on **OK**.

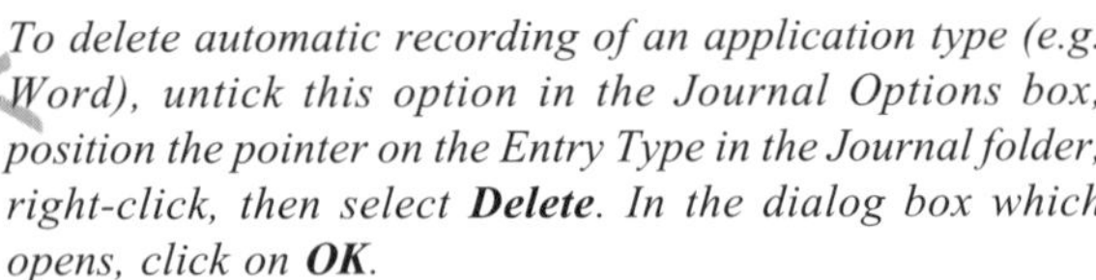

*To delete automatic recording of an application type (e.g. Word), untick this option in the Journal Options box, position the pointer on the Entry Type in the Journal folder, right-click, then select **Delete**. In the dialog box which opens, click on **OK**.*

JOURNAL VIEWS

The Journal folder offers several views for displaying a list of your Journal entries. To modify the Journal view, click on **View,** then **Current View**. Select the type of view in the drop-down menu. SeeTable 8.2 for the various views and their descriptions.

Table 8.2: Views in the Journal folder (see Figure 8.9).

View mode	Description
By type	Default view. Shows entries by type and in chronological order. To open the list, click on the + button opposite the type desired; simply point to an entry to see its contents.
By contact	Displays the name of each contact selected in Journal Entry. Click on the + button opposite the desired contact to open the Entry List for it.
By category	Displays the Journal entries by category. Click on the + button opposite the desired category to open the Entry List for it.
Entry List	Displays the entries in a table with indicators allowing you to sort or group the entries.
Last Seven Days	Displays the entries of the past week in a table with indicators allowing you to sort or group the entries.
Phone Calls	Displays the Journal entries corresponding to a phone call in chronological order.

*When you change the view, a dialog box asks you whether you want to save the modified view settings. Click on **OK**.*

To group Journal entries:

1. Click on the indicator by which you want to group, and hold the button down.

   A greyed field appears.

2. Drag to the greyed field and release the button.

*To ungroup your entries, place the pointer on the grouping indicator in the greyed field, then right-click and select **Do not Group by This Field**.*

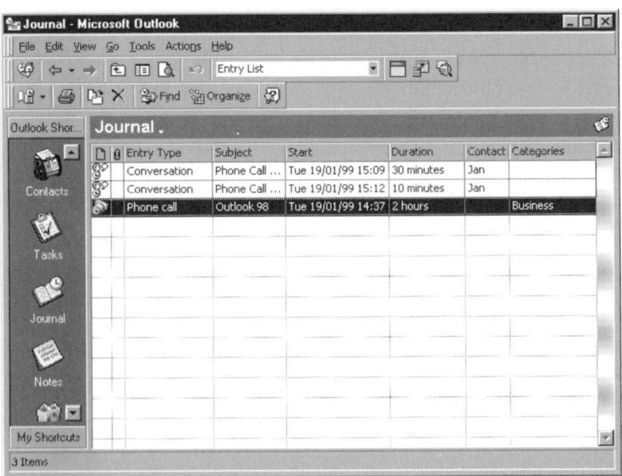

Figure 8.9: The Journal Folder indicators in the header of the various views allow you to group or sort Journal entries

Table 8.3: Journal folder keyboard shortcuts.

Action	Keyboard shortcut
In the Journal folder	
New entry	**Ctrl-N**
Delete an entry	**Ctrl-D**
In the Journal Entry box	
Record an entry	**Ctrl-S**
Delete an entry	**Ctrl-D**
Print an entry	**Ctrl-P**
Close the box	**Alt-F4**
New entry	**Ctrl-N**

Table 8.4: Journal folder symbols.

Symbol	Description
	Note
	Phone call
	Task
	Attachment to the Journal entry

NOTES FOLDER

This folder is the electronic equivalent of 'post-it notes'. These notes are useful for storing information such as instructions or text which can be used in other items or documents.

Notes created in this way can stay open on screen while you work, which allows you to refer to them at any time.

To open the Notes folder, click on the **Notes** icon in the Outlook Shortcuts bar.

Standard toolbar of the Notes folder

In addition to the icons common to all the standard toolbars, Table 8.5 lists the icons specific to the Notes toolbar.

Table 8.5: Icons specific to the Notes toolbar.

Icon	Description
	Opens a new note
Large Icons	Displays the note and its text in a box located underneath (default view)
Small Icons	Displays the note and its text on a line to the right of the note
List	Displays the notes in the form of a list

Clicking on an icon in the toolbar activates its function.

CREATING NOTES

To create a note:

1. Click on **New Note** in the toolbar.

   A small yellow box is displayed (see Figure 8.10).

2. Enter the text of your note.

3. To close it, click on the **Close** button of the Note box.

   Your note is displayed in the folder (see Figure 8.11).

You can enter as much information as you want: the lines of text wrap automatically and there is no limit to the content.

When you have a lot of text to enter, you can increase the size of the note box to view all the text.

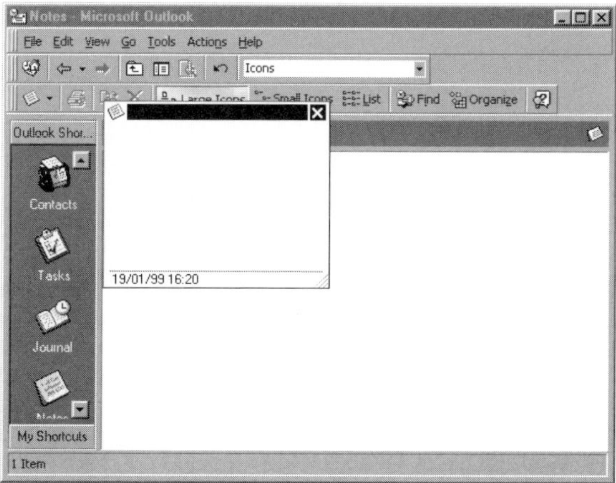

Figure 8.10: A box is displayed, in which you enter your note

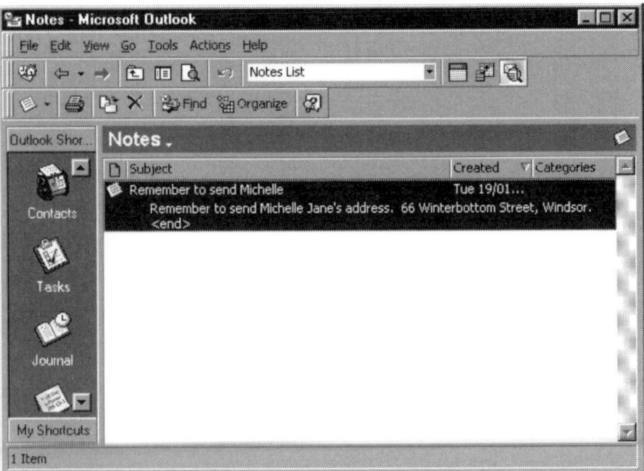

Figure 8.11: The note created is displayed in the Notes screen

To increase the box size:

1. Place the pointer on the edge of the note.

   Arrows appear at either end of the pointer.

2. Click and, keeping the mouse button depressed, drag until the required size is obtained.

To modify a note:

1. Double-click on the desired note and make your changes.
2. When you have finished, click on the **Close** button.

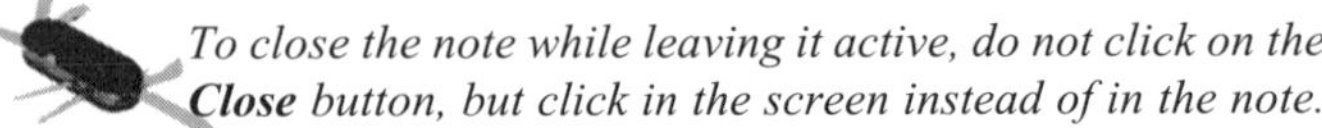

*To close the note while leaving it active, do not click on the **Close** button, but click in the screen instead of in the note.*

MANAGING AND MODIFYING NOTES

You will now learn how to manage and modify your notes.

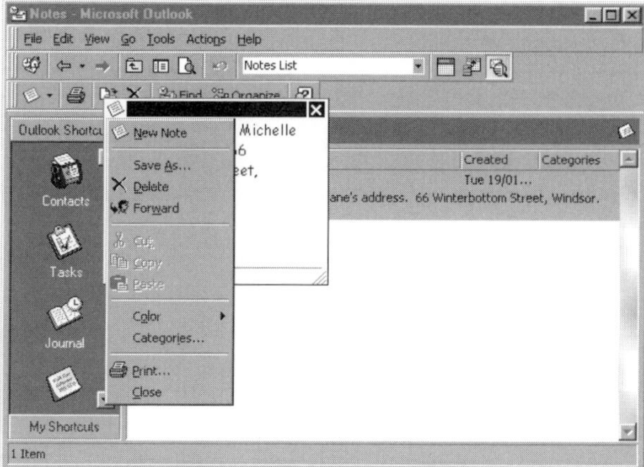

Figure 8.12: The context-sensitive menu of a note

Managing notes

Outlook offers several options for managing your notes. These options are accessible from the context-sensitive menu of the note (see Figure 8.12).

To open the context-sensitive menu of a note:

1. After opening the note concerned, click on the **System** button.
2. Select the command desired.

Table 8.6: The commands of the context-sensitive menu of a note.

Command	Description
New note	Open a new note without closing the current note
Save As	Open the Save As box which allows you to save the note in a folder or file

Table 8.6: The commands of the context-sensitive menu of a note (cont.).

Command	Description
Delete	Deletes the note
Cut, Copy, Paste	Selects the text for copying or pasting in the clipboard
Color	Selects another colour for the box of your note; five colours are available
Categories	Selects a category for the note
Print	Prints the content of the note
Close	Closes the note

The colour function allows you to colour the notes according to their category, type, etc. For example: blue for notes concerning your customers, yellow for notes concerning your sales prospects, and so on.

Modifying notes

Outlook allows you to choose the font, colour and size of your notes.

To set the parameters of the note:

1. In the Notes folder, click on **Tools**, then **Options**.
2. In the **Preferences** tab, click on the **Notes Options** button (see Figure 8.13).
3. Make your choice, then click on **OK**.

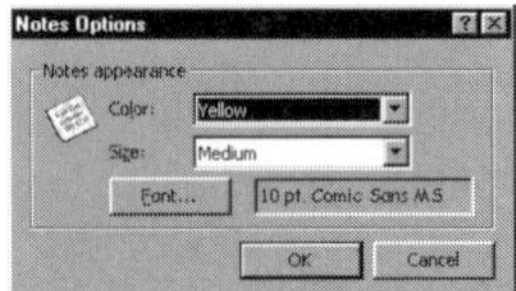

Figure 8.13: The note parameters

VIEWS

As in the other Outlook folders, the Notes folder offers a number of views for listing your notes. See Table 8.7 for their description.

Table 8.7: Views in the Notes folder (see Figure 8.14).

View mode	Description
Icons	Default view. Shows notes as icons with the beginning of the message as the title.
Notes List	Displays all the notes as a list, showing the title and note contents in the Subject column, the creation date and time, and the category.
Last Seven Days	Displays all the notes created in the preceding week by subject, creation date, and category.
By category	Displays the notes by category. Click on the + button of the desired category to display the notes.
By color	Displays the notes by colour. Click on the + button of the desired colour to display the notes.

To change the Notes view mode:

1. Click on **View**, then **Current View**.
2. Select the view you want from the drop-down menu.

When you change the view, a dialog box asks you whether you want to save modified view settings. Click on ***OK***.

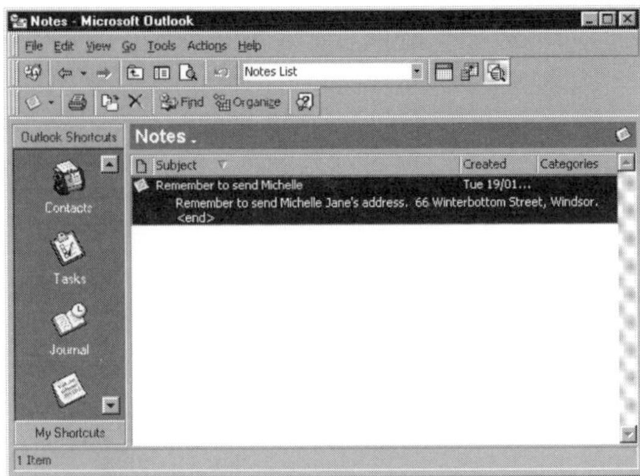

Figure 8.14: The Notes folder indicators in the headers of the different views, allowing you to group or sort your notes

To group or sort your notes:

1. Click on the desired indicator to group the notes and hold the button down.
2. Drag to the greyed field and release the button.

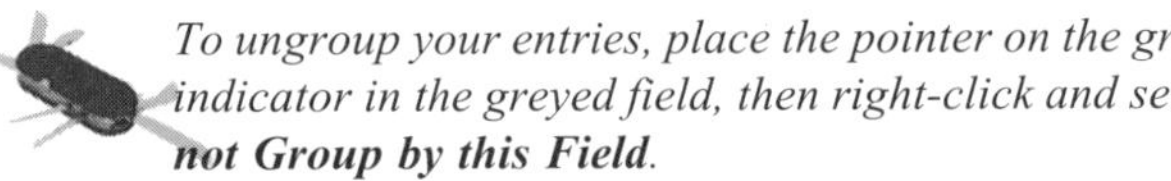

*To ungroup your entries, place the pointer on the grouping indicator in the greyed field, then right-click and select **Do not Group by this Field**.*

Table 8.8: Keyboard shortcuts of the Notes folder.

Action	Keyboard shortcut
New note	**Ctrl-N**
Delete a note	**Ctrl-D**

Hour 9

Organisation and assignment

The contents for this hour

- Planning a meeting
- Replying to an invitation to a meeting
- Assigning tasks
- Receiving tasks

Planning a meeting

In the Calendar folder, you will be able to create and organise meetings using the **Attendee Availability** tab as it displays the available and occupied time slots for the people invited, and the resources to be used. The meeting planning function is accessible from the Calendar folder.

Resources are items needed for your meeting such as room, overhead projector, film, etc.

To plan a meeting:

1. In the Calendar folder, click on the **New Appointment** button in the standard toolbar.

   The Appointment box is displayed (see Figure 9.1).

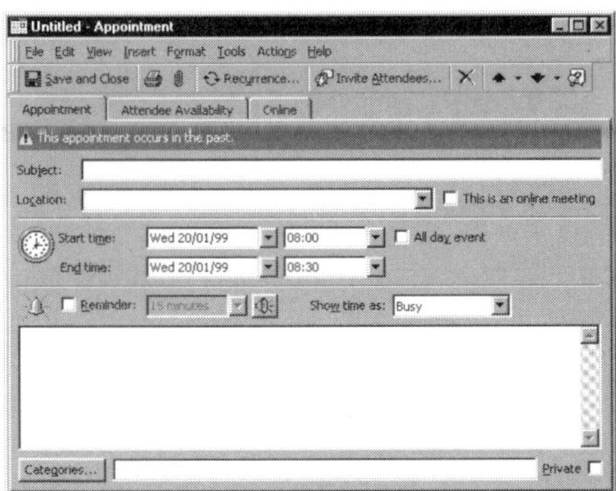

Figure 9.1: The Appointment box

2. Click on the **Attendee Availability** tab.
3. Click on the **Invite Others** button or enter the names of attendees in the list.

In the list of attendees, you can only enter the names of people in your address books. Outlook will not be able to send invitations to meetings or check the availability of the attendees if they are not in your address books.

The Select Attendees and Resources box is displayed (see Figure 9.2).

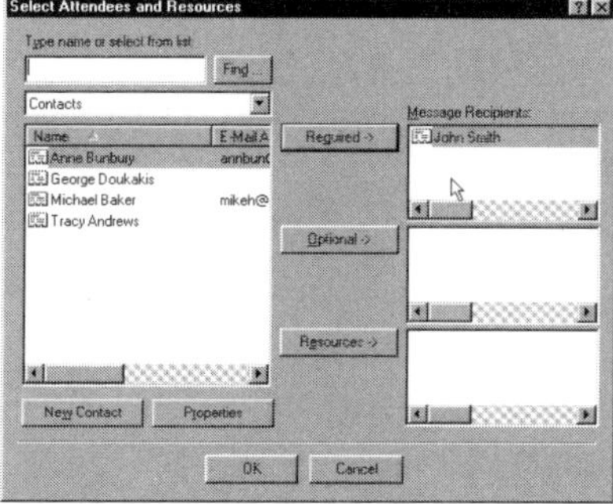

Figure 9.2: Using the Select Attendees and Resources box, you choose those to be invited to the meeting

4. Select the Address Book of your choice.
5. Click on the desired name in the list.
6. Click on **Required** if this person is indispensable or click on **Optional** if their presence is not vital.
7. Repeat steps 4 and 5 for each of the attendees.
8. Click on **OK** when you have finished.

   The **Attendee Availability** tab is displayed (see Figure 9.3).

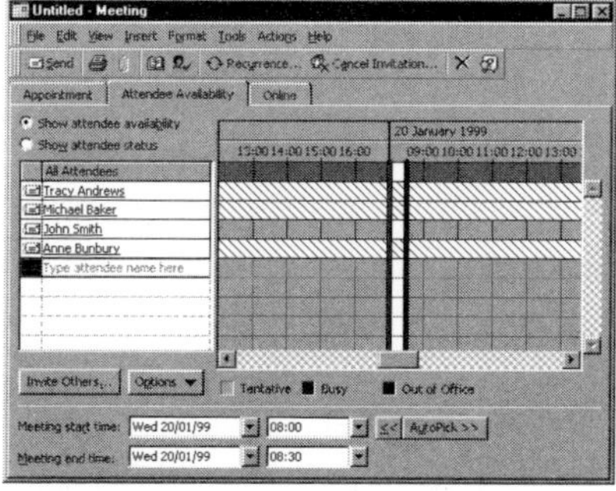

Figure 9.3: The Attendee Availability tab displays the list of attendees

9. Click on the first name in the list and check the person's availability. Do the same for all attendees.
10. Click on the icon for each attendee and select **Send meeting to this attendee**.
11. Click on the **Appointment** tab (see Figure 9.4).

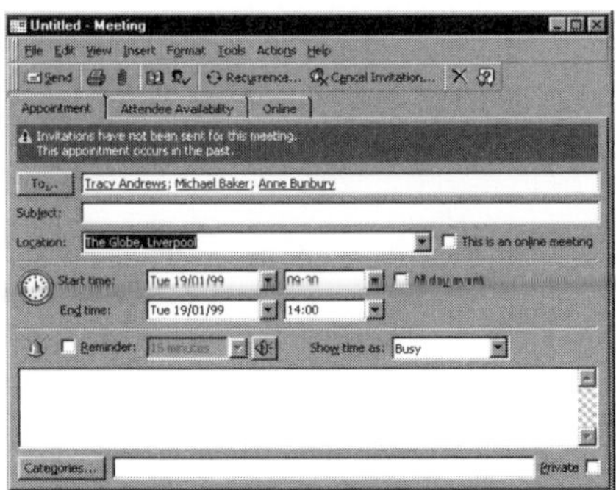

Figure 9.4: The Appointment tab allows you to define the options for your meeting

12. Indicate the options desired (subject, location, text, etc.).

    Outlook automatically sends an invitation message to each of the attendees.

Adding attendees

You may want to invite other people. If so, you must add them to the list of attendees.

To add attendees for a meeting:

1. In the Calendar, select the date of the meeting in the Calendar pane.
2. Double-click on the blue field of the relevant meeting.
3. Click on the **Attendee Availability** tab, then on **Invite Others**.

4. Click on the desired name in the list, then click on **Required** or **Optional** and on **OK**.

   In the **Attendee Availability** tab, all your attendees are displayed in the list.

5. Click on the icon opposite each attendee, and select **Send meeting to this attendee** or **Don't Send meeting to this attendee** depending on whether or not they have already been notified (see Figure 9.5).

   Outlook sends an invitation message to all new attendees.

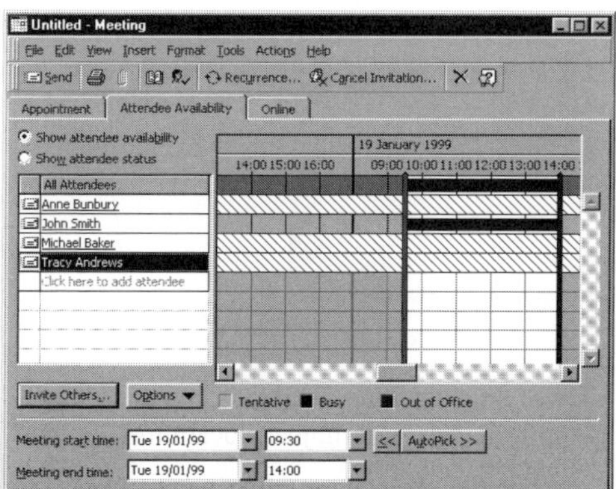

Figure 9.5: Outlook selects the attendees to whom you are not sending an invitation

Checking replies to my invitations

Having planned the meeting, you must follow up the invitations in order to find out who will be attending. Replies will appear in the form of messages in your Inbox. Outlook also allows you to directly verify attendee availability.

To check the replies of your invitees:

1. In the Calendar folder, after selecting the relevant day, double-click on the blue field of the meeting.

2. Click on the **Attendee Availability** tab, then click on the **Show attendee status** option.

3. When you have finished, click on **File**, then select **Close**.

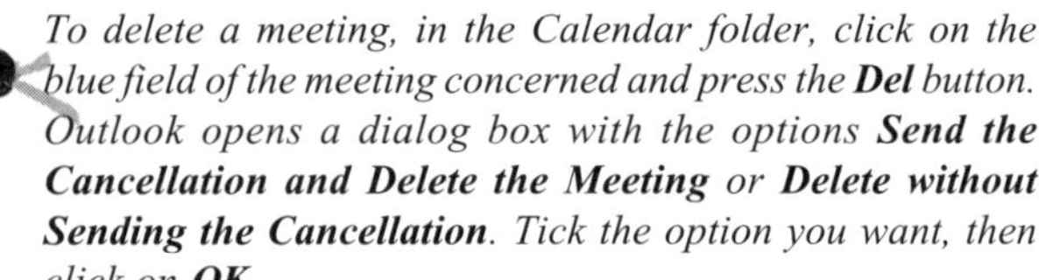

*To delete a meeting, in the Calendar folder, click on the blue field of the meeting concerned and press the **Del** button. Outlook opens a dialog box with the options **Send the Cancellation and Delete the Meeting** or **Delete without Sending the Cancellation**. Tick the option you want, then click on **OK**.*

Modifying a meeting after it has been planned

If you want to change the time or venue of your meeting after the invitees have already received an invitation, follow the steps below.

1. In the Calendar folder, after selecting the desired day in the Calendar pane, double-click on the blue field of the meeting concerned in the Schedule.

2. Click on the Appointment tab and make the necessary changes; you could insert text in the appropriate field to explain the reasons for the change. This text will be sent by Outlook with the cancellation message.

3. Click on the **Attendee Availability** tab.

4. Opposite each attendee, click on the icon and select the option **Send meeting to this attendee**.

   Outlook will send each attendee a meeting modification message.

Replying to an invitation to a meeting

Imagine that you have received a message inviting you to a meeting. You must now answer.

To optimise management of your invitations, click on **Office Assistant**.

To reply to a meeting request:

1. Double-click on the message concerned in the Inbox.

   The Message box opens, indicating the location, subject and date of the meeting (see Figure 9.6).

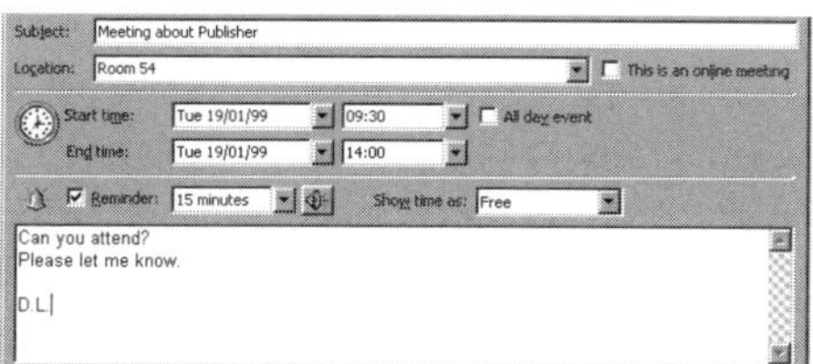

Figure 9.6: The Message box containing a description of the meeting

2. Click on your choice in the toolbar (acceptance, provisional acceptance or rejection).

   Office Assistant is activated and displays a message.

3. Click on the desired option.
4. Enter your text (if you have chosen Modify Reply Before Sending).

   Outlook sends the modifications.

Managing your availability

Outlook can optimise the management of your time for all the invitations you receive. These options are accessible in the Options dialog box.

To configure the advanced scheduling options:

1. Within a folder, click on **Tools**, then select **Options**.
2. Click on the **Calendar Options** button.
3. Click on the **Free/Busy Options** button (see Figure 9.7).

   Table 9.1 describes the different advanced scheduling options.

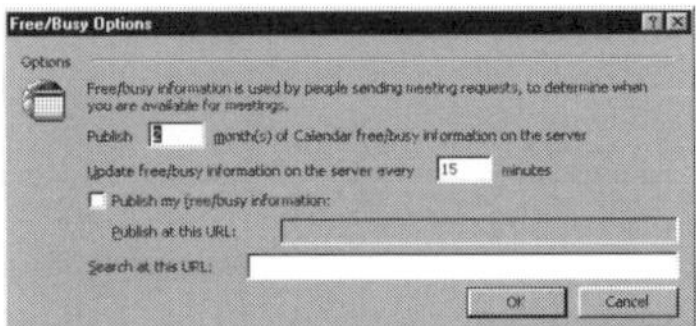

Figure 9.7: The Free/Busy Options box

4. Tick the desired options (see Table 9.1).
5. Click on **OK**.
6. Click on the **Resource Scheduling** button.
7. Tick the desired options.
8. Click on **OK**.

Table 9.1: Advanced scheduling options.

Option	Description
Automatically accept meeting requests and process cancellations	Allows you to automatically reply to your invitations when you accept and allows you to send a negative reply when you are not available
Automatically decline conflicting meeting requests	Allows you to automatically refuse all meetings scheduled for the same time as another meeting or when you are not available in the Calendar

Table 9.1: Advanced scheduling options (cont.).

Option	Description
Automatically decline recurring meeting requests	Allows you to automatically refuse recurring meetings
Publish *x* month(s) of Calendar free/busy information on the server	Allows you to indicate the number of months accessible by other server users when they want to view your Calendar
Update free/busy information on the server every *x* minutes	Allows you to indicate the update frequency of your Calendar on the server so that your up-to-date Calendar can be viewed by other users

Assigning tasks

In Hour 7, you learned how to create tasks corresponding to each of the jobs you have to carry out. In the Tasks folder, you can record the development of your tasks, note statistics, store their actual cost, etc.

Outlook allows you to assign a task, and to monitor it afterwards.

When you assign a task which you have created, you lose ownership of it, i.e. you can no longer modify its details, such as its due date, percentage completion, etc. However, you can receive progress reports.

To assign a task which has not yet been created:

1. Click on the **Tasks** icon in the Outlook Shortcuts bar.
2. Click on **File**, then select **New**, drag to open the drop-down menu and click on **Task Request**.

The Task box is displayed (see Figure 9.8).

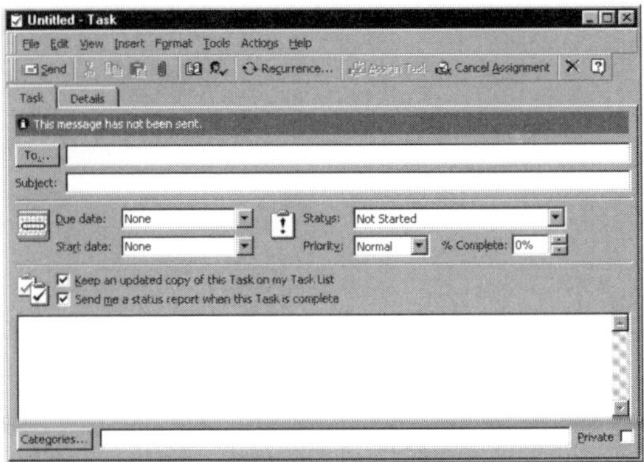

Figure 9.8: The Task tab in the Task box

3. Click on the **Task** tab (if necessary).
4. Click on **To**.

   The Select Task Recipient box is displayed (see Figure 9.9).

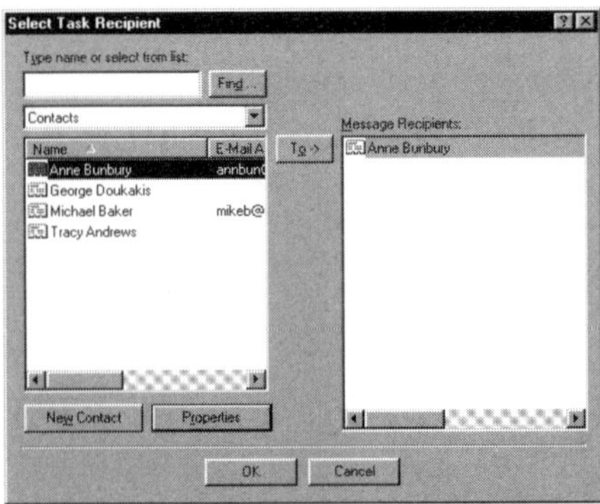

Figure 9.9: Choose the person to whom you want to assign the task

5. Select the Address Book of your choice.
6. Click on the name you want in the list of names.
7. Click on **To**.
8. Click on **OK**.
9. In the Task box, enter the subject, due date, status and any instructions, depending on the task or message you are assigning.
10. Click on **Send** in the toolbar.

    You can also assign a task which has already been created.

To do this:

1. In the Tasks folder, place the pointer on the task concerned and right-click.
2. In the context-sensitive menu, click on **Assign Task** (see Figure 9.10).

   The Task box is displayed (see Figure 9.11).

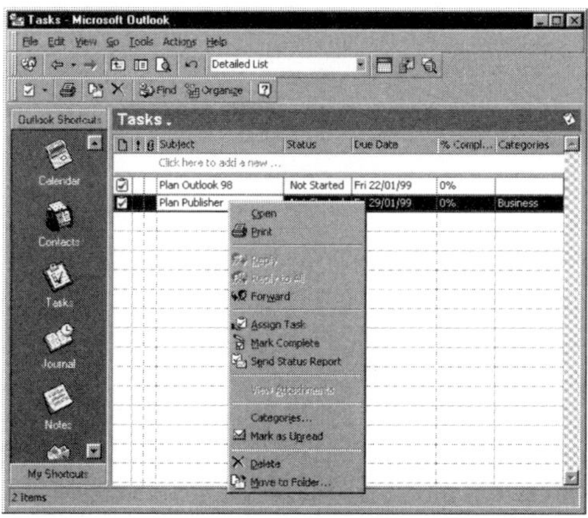

Figure 9.10: The context-sensitive menu of a task

Figure 9.11: Task options

3. Click on the Task tab (if necessary).
4. Click on **To**.

   The Select Task Recipient box is displayed (see Figure 9.9).
5. Select the address book of your choice.
6. Click on the name you want in the list of names.
7. Click on **To**.
8. Click on **OK**.
9. In the text field, enter the instructions relating to the task you are assigning.
10. Click on **Send** in the toolbar.

To find out whether your task has been accepted, check the message corresponding to this task in the Inbox.

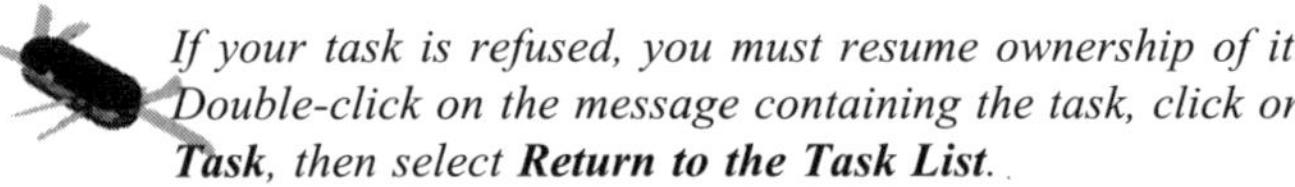

*If your task is refused, you must resume ownership of it. Double-click on the message containing the task, click on **Task**, then select **Return to the Task List**.*

Monitoring assigned tasks

As already mentioned, a task no longer belongs to you when it has been assigned: you can no longer alter the due date, progress, etc. On the other hand, you can retain a copy of it and receive progress reports on it.

To keep a copy of the assigned task and receive progress reports:

1. When creating the task, click on the desired task option (see Figure 9.11).

2. Tick the **Keep an updated copy of this Task on my Task List** option to keep a copy of the task.
3. Tick the **Send me a status report when this Task is complete** option to receive a progress report on the task.
4. Click on **Send**.

Viewing assigned tasks

To remind you of all tasks, Outlook provides a special view.
To see tasks you have assigned:

1. In the Tasks folder, click on **View**, **Current View**.
2. Select **Assignment**.

RECEIVING TASKS

When you receive and accept a task request, you become the owner of the task, and continue to be its owner until the completion of the task. But you can refuse it or assign it to somebody else. To do this, you must choose an option as soon as the request is received.

The different task reception options are as follows:

- **Accept.** When you accept a task, you become its owner. You can then modify its due date, its status, etc. Changes you make will also be reflected in any copy the sender has retained. By accepting a task, you can send comments to the person who assigned it to you.
- **Refuse.** When you refuse a task, it is returned to its sender. You can attach comments to it.
- **Assign a task.** You can refuse a task and, instead of returning it to its sender, assign it to a third person. In this case, you may retain a copy, by configuring the options as indicated above.

Accepting a task request

Imagine that you have received a message assigning a task to you. To optimise management of your reply, click on Office Assistant in the toolbar.

To accept the task:

1. Double-click on the message concerned in the Inbox (see Figure 9.12).

Figure 9.12: The message containing the task request is displayed

2. Click on **Accept** in the toolbar.
3. Click on the option of your choice:
   - If you have chosen the **Send Reply Now** option, Outlook automatically sends a positive reply to the sender of the task.
   - If you have chosen the **Do Not Send Reply** option, click on **File**, then select **Close**.
   - If you have chosen the **Modify Reply Before Sending** option, enter your reply in the text field.
4. Click on **Send** in the toolbar.

Refusing a task request

Imagine that you have received a message assigning a task to you. To optimise management of your reply, click on Office Assistant in the toolbar.

To refuse the task:

1. Double-click on the message concerned in the Inbox.
2. Click on **Refuse** in the toolbar.
3. Click on the option of your choice:
   - If you have chosen the **Send Reply Now** option, Outlook automatically sends a negative reply to the sender of the task.
   - If you have chosen the **Do Not Send Reply** option, click on **File**, then select **Close**.
   - If you have chosen the **Modify Reply Before Sending** option, enter your reply in the text field.
4. Click on **Send** in the toolbar.

Assigning a task request

Imagine that you have received a message assigning a task to you. To optimise management of your reply, click on Office Assistant in the toolbar.

To assign the task to another person:

1. Double-click on the message concerned in the Inbox.
2. Click on **Assign a Task** in the toolbar.
3. Click on **To**.
4. Select the desired Address Book.
5. Select the desired name in the list and click on **To**, then on **OK**.

6. Enter any comments in the text field.
7. Click on **Send** in the toolbar.

Table 9.2: Keyboard shortcuts for Hour 9.

Action	Keyboard shortcut
In the Meeting box	
Send	**Ctrl-Enter**
Close	**Alt-F4**
In the Task box	
Send	**Ctrl-Enter**
Close	**Alt-F4**
In the Tasks folder	
New task request	**Ctrl-Shift-U**

Table 9.3: Meeting organisation and task assignment symbols.

Symbol	Description
	Acceptance of meeting request
	Provisional acceptance of meeting request
	Cancellation of meeting
	Refusal of meeting request

Table 9.3: Meeting organisation and task assignment symbols (cont.).

Symbol	Description
	In the Inbox, meeting symbol
	Task accepted
	Task refused
	Task assigned to another person
	Task assigned to you

Hour 10

Printing and Inserting files into an Outlook item

THE CONTENTS FOR THIS HOUR

- Page setup
- Print preview
- Printing
- Inserting files or objects into an Outlook item

In this hour, you will learn how to print various Outlook items, how to customise your printing, how to choose a page setup for one or more items, how to change the page orientation, and so on. You will see how to optimise your printing operations and how to customise them according to your requirements.

To print an item:

1. Whatever folder you are in, click on the item to select it.
2. Click on the **Print** icon in the toolbar.

   Outlook opens the Print dialog box.
3. Click on **OK**.

   Your item will be printed.

Page setup

In each folder, Outlook offers different views associated with the print styles you select in the Page Setup box.

Before choosing the page setup or printing items, you must select them.

You can choose:

- **Selection of one item.** Whatever folder you are in, simply click on the item to select it.
- **Selection of several items.** Whatever folder you are in, click on the first item to be selected, then hold down the **Ctrl** key and click on the second item, third item, and so on.
- **Selection of all the items.** Whatever folder you are in, click on the first item to be selected, place the pointer on the last item to be selected, hold the **Shift** key down and click.

Choosing a print style

The print style is actually a combination of several predefined printing options. For example, the table style offers printing in columns and lines with portrait orientation and a margin.

Different print styles

By default, Outlook offers a number of print styles for each folder. Table 10.1 describes each of the styles.

Table 10.1: Default print styles in Outlook.

Print style	Folders offering this style	Description
Table	All folders	Provides data in lines and columns with portrait orientation and a margin
Memo	All folders	Provides data with a page header and footer, portrait orientation and a margin
Daily	Calendar	Provides a day's data on one page with portrait orientation and a margin
Weekly	Calendar	Provides a week's data on one page with portrait orientation and a margin
Monthly	Calendar	Provides a month's data on one page with portrait orientation and a margin
Tri-fold	Calendar	Provides data with landscape orientation and a margin. The page displays the daily calendar, task list and weekly calendar

Table 10.1: Default print styles in Outlook (cont.).

Print style	Folders offering this style	Description
Card	Contacts	Provides two columns with page header and footer, portrait orientation and a margin. It also provides an alphabetic index
Medium Booklet	Contacts	Provides four columns with alphabetic index, landscape orientation and a margin
Small Booklet	Contacts	Provides one column over half the page with alphabetic index in portrait orientation and a margin
Phone Directory	Contacts	Provides one column on the whole page with portrait orientation and a margin

These choices are accessible according to the selected folder and view.

- Contacts folder:
  - **Address Cards and Detailed Address Cards.** Card, Medium Booklet, Small Booklet, Memo and Phone Directory.
  - **All other views.** Table, Memo and Phone Directory.

- Calendar folder:
  - **Day/Week/Month.** Daily, Weekly, Monthly, Tri-fold, Memo.
  - **All other views.** Table and Memo.
- Journal folder:
  - **Entry List and Last Seven Days.** Table and Memo.
  - **All other views.** Memo.
- Tasks folder:
  - **Task Timeline.** Memo.
  - **All other views.** Table and Memo.
- Notes folder:
  - **Icons.** Memo.
  - **All other views.** Memo and Table.
- Inbox folder:
  - **Message Timeline.** Memo.
  - **All other views.** Table and Memo.

To choose a print style:

1. Select the view type in the folder or select the items to be made up into pages.
2. Click on **File**, then select **Page Setup**, drag to the right of the command to open the drop-down menu and select the desired style (see Figure 10.1).

   The Page Setup box opens (see Figure 10.2).

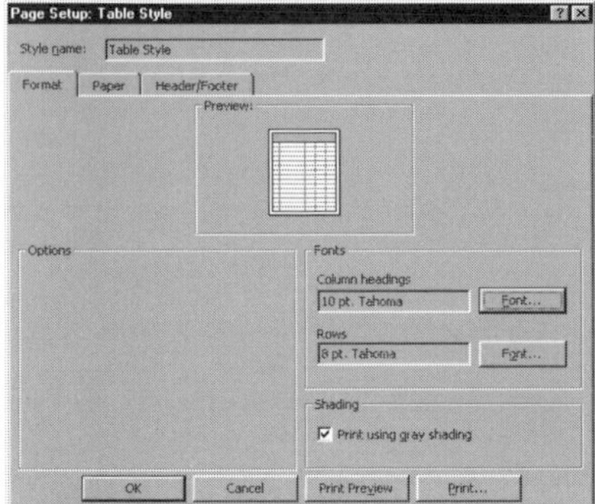

Figure 10.1: The Page Setup box, here showing Table Style

Choosing a page setup

Page setup only affects printing, i.e. the items you are printing, not the layouts or views in the program itself.

You have selected your item or chosen the view in the folder of your choice. When you choose a print style, the Page Setup box opens. By default, the Format tab is displayed (see Figure 10.2).

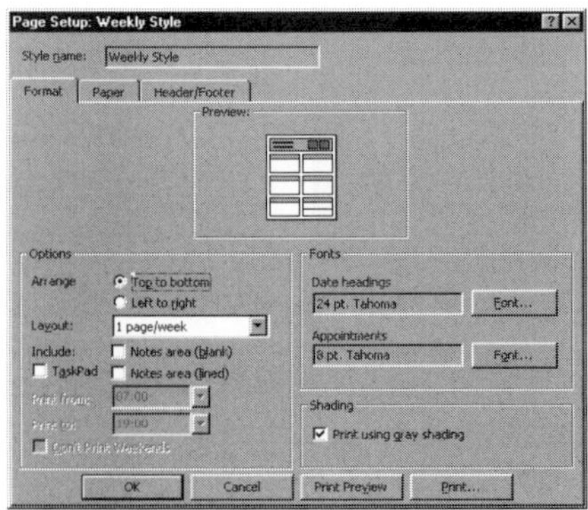

Figure 10.2: The Format tab of the Page Setup box

*The **Format** tab of the Page Setup box varies depending on the style chosen, and offers options in keeping with this style.*

For a page setup in Memo style:

1. In the desired folder, click on **View,** then **Current View** and select the desired view.
2. Choose the item to be made up into pages, click on **File**, then select **Page Setup** and drag to open the drop-down menu, from which you select **Memo Style**. From here, you make your choices for printing your items.
3. When you have made your choices, click on the **Paper** tab and make your choices (see Figure 10.3).

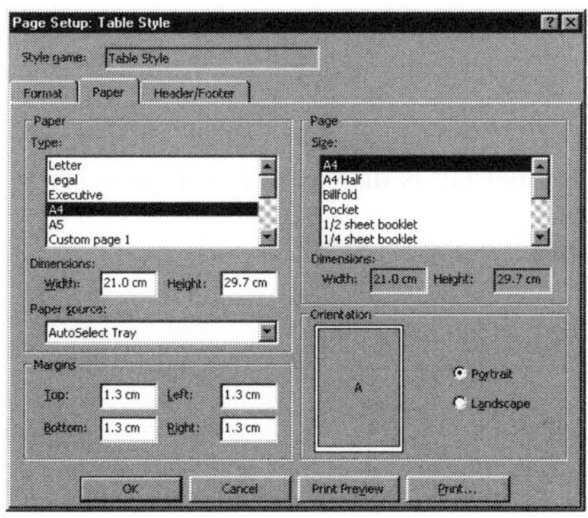

Figure 10.3: The Paper tab in the Page Setup box

Portrait orientation means 21 cm wide × 29.7 cm high. Landscape orientation means 29.7 cm wide × 21 cm high.

4. Click on the **Header/Footer** tab.
5. Click in one of the header areas and enter your header.
6. Click in one of the footer areas and enter your footer.
7. Click on **OK**.

While 'paper' means what is loaded into the printer, 'page' means the area on the paper which will be printed. You can print several pages on a single sheet of paper. For example, when you print out contacts, you will have several Address Cards on the same sheet of paper.

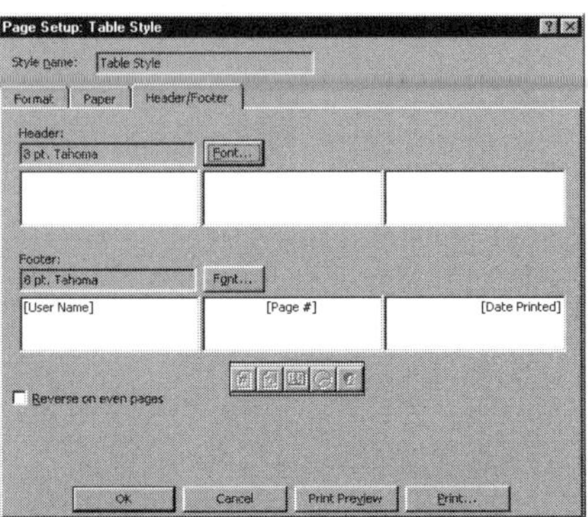

Figure 10.4: The Header/Footer tab in the Page Setup box

*The **Print Preview** button of the box displays the whole page with the page setup you have defined.*

For a weekly style layout:

1. In the Calendar folder, click on **View,** then **Current View** and select the **Day/Week/Month** view.
2. Click on **File**, then select **Page Setup** and drag to open the drop-down menu, from which you select **Weekly Style**.

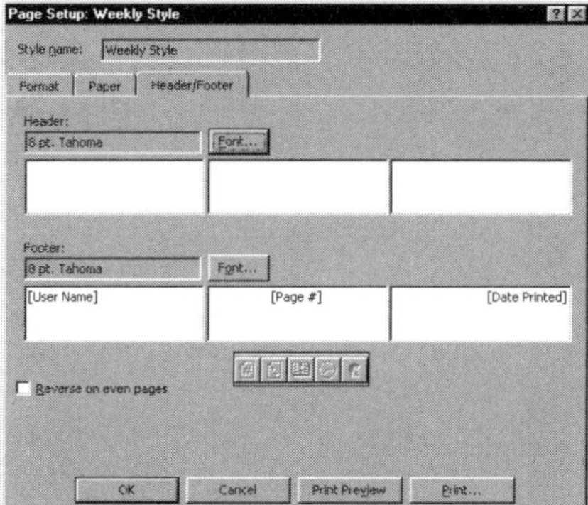

Figure 10.5: The Page Setup box for Weekly Style

The **Paper** and **Header/Footer** tabs are common to all styles (see Figures 10.3 and 10.4).

3. When you have made your choices, click on **OK**.

PRINT PREVIEW

It can be useful to see what you are going to print before starting the print operation, by using the Print Preview command.

There are two ways to open Print Preview:

- In the folder of the item or items to be printed, click on **Print Preview** in the toolbar.
- Click on **Print Preview** in the Page Setup box (see Figure 10.6).

To use the zoom:

1. Click on the **Zoom** icon in the toolbar.
2. Move the pointer to the page area you want to enlarge and click on it.
3. To exit from zoom, click on any point in the page.

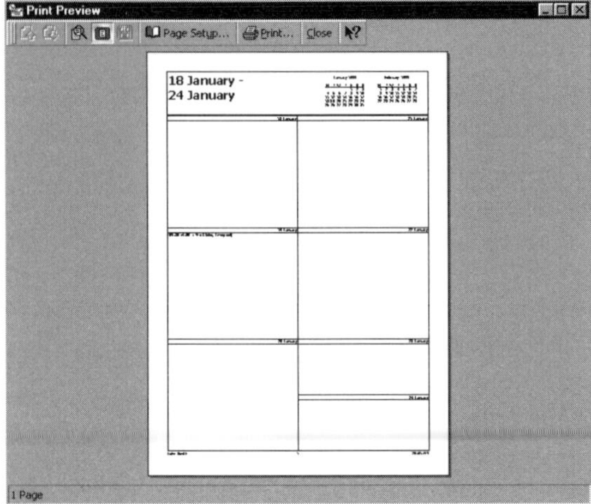

Figure 10.6: Print Preview

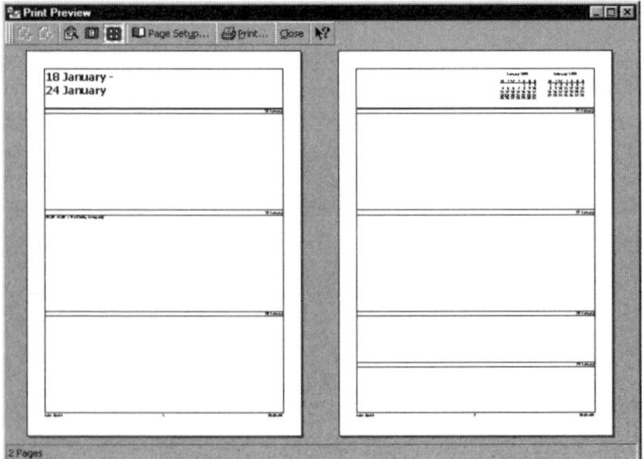

Figure 10.7: Print Preview allows you to display several pages on screen

PRINTING

Having made your choice of styles and page setup, you can print your items. Remember that you can also print without creating page setups, after selecting one or more items.

To print:

1. Click on the **Print** icon in the toolbar of the folder you are in.

   The Print box opens (see Figure 10.8).

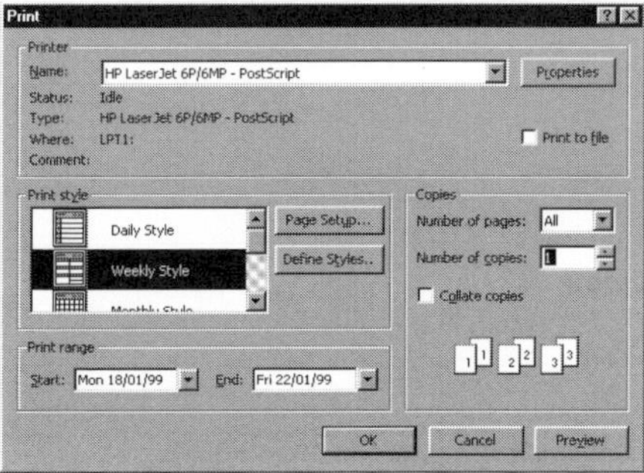

Figure 10.8: The Print box allows you to choose from print options offered by Outlook

2. Make your choices.

   For a description of the print options, see Table 10.2.

Table 10.2: Print box options.

Option	Description
Name	Click on the arrow and select the printer
Properties	Click on **Properties** and make the various choices (paper source, graphics, recto-verso, resolution, colour, etc.)

Table 10.2: Print box options (cont.).

Option	Description
Print style	Click on the arrow to scroll up or down the list, then select the style of your choice
Page Setup	Click on **Page Setup** to open the box, make your choices and click on **OK**
Define Styles	Click on **Define Styles** to choose a style
Number of pages	Click on the arrow and select the option desired (All, Even or Odd)
Number of copies	Click on the arrow and select the number of copies desired
Collate copies	Tick the box to collate the copies
Print range	Tick the desired box to print the selected items

3. When you have made your choices, click on **OK**.

   Outlook starts the print operation.

Print attachments

You may receive messages, tasks or meeting requests with files attached to them. You can also send messages with file attachments.

To print the attachments:

1. Click on the item which contains the attachments (see Figure 10.9).

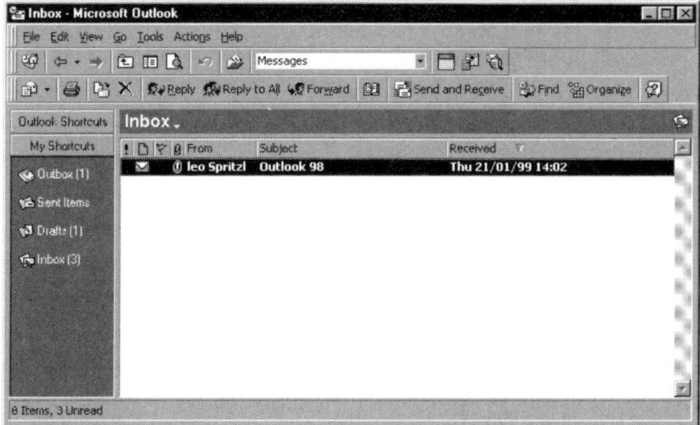

Figure 10.9: The Inbox folder containing a message with an attachment

2. Click on **File**, then select **Print**.

3. In the **Print Style** field, click on **Memo Style**.

4. Tick the **Print attached files with item(s)** box.

5. After making your choices in the various options, click on **OK**.

You can also print an attachment from its application:

1. In the item concerned, double-click on the attachment; it will open in its own application.

2. Click on **File**, then select **Print**.

3. In the Print box, select your choice (number of copies, printer, orientation, etc.) and then click on **OK**.

4. Click on **File**, then select **Exit** in the attachment application.

5. Returning to Outlook, click on **File**, then select **Exit**.

Printing a specified number of days in the Calendar

To print the Calendar, certain print options are offered:

- **Daily.** Prints the day displayed.
- **Weekly.** Prints the week displayed.
- **Monthly.** Prints the month displayed.

You can choose one of these styles, which will print the number of days corresponding to the choice specified (one day, seven days, 28, 29, 30 or 31 days).

To print a specified number of days:

1. In the Calendar folder, click on **File**, then select **Print**.
2. In the **Print style** field, choose the style desired.
3. In the **Start** field, enter the first day to be printed.
4. In the **End** field, enter the last day to be printed.
5. Click on **OK**.

Printing the address of a contact on an envelope or label

To send a large number of envelopes to be sent to your contacts, you can print labels or envelopes, which will save you a lot of time.

Two conditions are necessary for this operation:

- a knowledge of Microsoft Word; and
- the Contacts folder must appear in the Outlook Address Book.

To print the address of a contact on an envelope or label, proceed as follows:

1. In Word, click on **Tools**, then select **Envelopes and Labels** (see Figure 10.10).

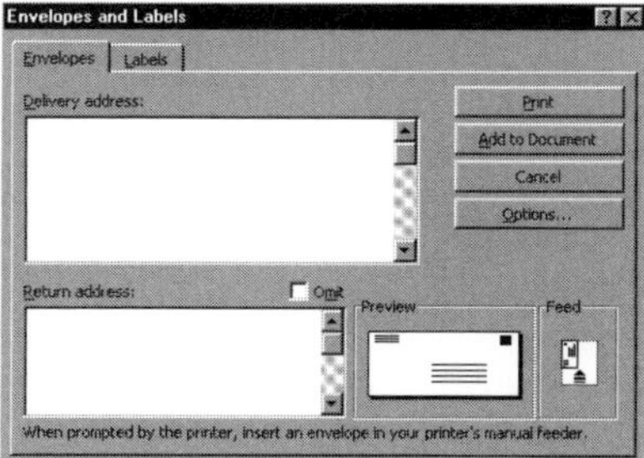

Figure 10.10: The Word Envelopes and Labels box

2. Click on the **Labels** or **Envelopes** tab.
3. Click on **Address Book**.
4. In the **Display the Names of** field, select the name of the folder in which the contact is located.
5. Double-click on the entry of your choice.
6. Click on **Print**.

Printing a view

You can print out everything appearing in the screen of your folder along with any indicators, symbols, etc. Table and phone directory are the styles which best lend themselves to this type of printing.

To print a view:

1. In the desired folder, and after selecting the view in Current View, click on **File** and then select **Print**.
2. In the Print box, select the print style desired (the Memo option is not available; it can only print one or more items, never a view).
3. Modify or indicate the options corresponding to your choice.
4. Click on **OK**.

INSERTING FILES OR OBJECTS INTO AN OUTLOOK ITEM

As you have already seen, you can incorporate a file from another application or an Outlook folder into an Outlook item. You can also insert an object (e.g. a drawing). You will now learn how to insert an existing file or an object without links: the data inserted is fixed and will not change if the source document is later altered. In Hour 11, you will learn how to insert linked items so that any modifications made to the file in its own application will be carried over to the file inserted into Outlook.

When you insert a file or a an object, a double-click is enough to open it. Similarly, if you insert a file into a message or an assigned task, the addressee need only double-click on the attachment to open it.

You can insert a file or an object into the following items:

- a message;
- a contact;
- a task;
- the Journal; or
- all Calendar items: appointments, meetings, task list.

To insert a file:

1. After displaying the desired folder, double-click on the item in which you want to insert a file.
2. Click on **Insert**, then **File** in the toolbar of the box you have just opened.

   The Insert File box is displayed (see Figure 10.11).
3. Select the drive and/or the folder containing the desired file.

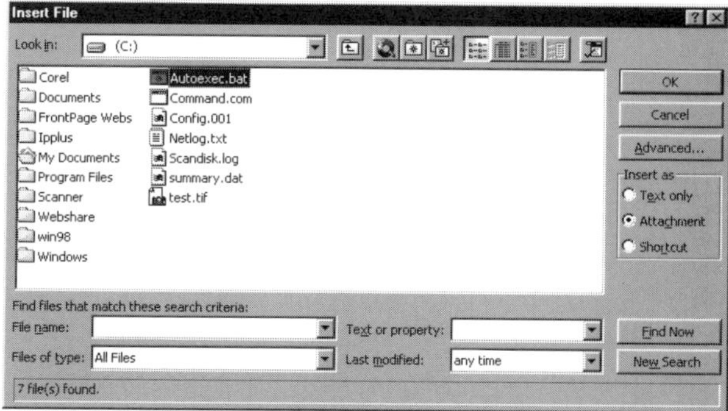

Figure 10.11: The Insert File box allows you to find the file you want to insert

4. Click on the file to be inserted, then click on **OK**.

   This file is displayed in the text field of the box of the item where you have inserted it (see Figure 10.12).

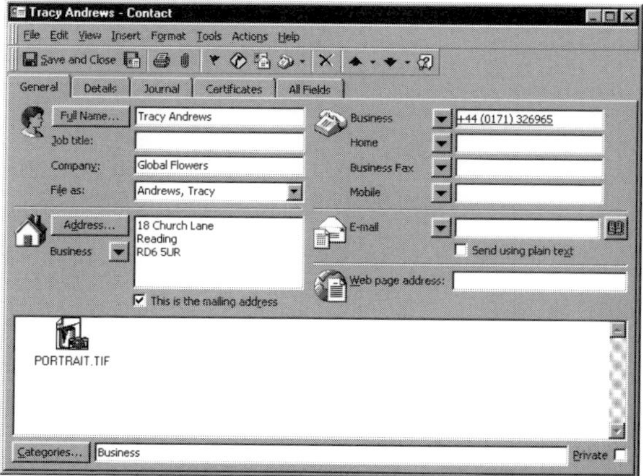

Figure 10.12: The inserted file is displayed as an icon in the text field

5. Click on **Save and Close** in the toolbar.

Don't forget that an inserted item is not a linked item! The inserted item will not be modified if its source file is modified.

To insert an object such as a drawing, a graphics object, etc., carry out the following steps:

1. After displaying the folder of your choice, double-click on the item into which you want to insert a file.
2. Locate the pointer in the text field of the box which has opened, and click.
3. Click on **Insert**, then select **Object** (see Figure 10.13).

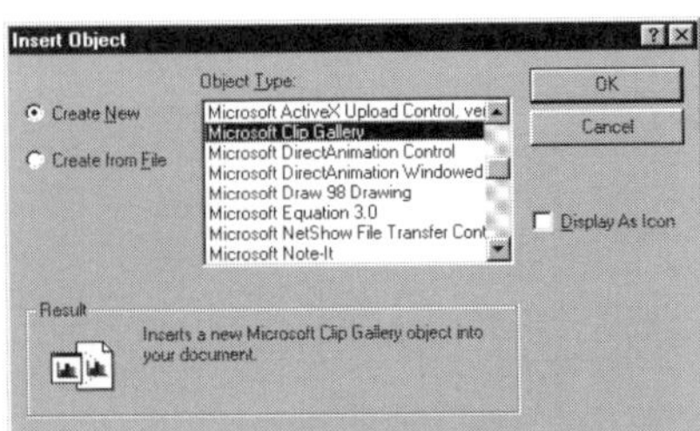

Figure 10.13: The Insert Object box

4. Double-click on **Microsoft Clip Gallery** (see Figure 10.14).
5. Select the category desired.
6. Click on the desired image.
7. Click on **Insert**.

   The chosen image is displayed in the text field of the box of the item in which you want to insert the image.

8. Click on **Save and Close**.

Figure 10.14: The Clip Gallery

Table 10.3: Keyboard shortcuts for Hour 10.

Action	Keyboard shortcut
Print	**Ctrl-P**

Hour 11

Organising items

The contents for this hour

- Saving items
- Finding items
- Linking items
- Using templates

Saving items

Outlook automatically saves certain items (such as receipt of messages and assignment of tasks) without any action on your part. For other functions (the creation of messages, creation of tasks, creation of appointments), you use the Save and Close command to save your items.

If you want to save an item to use it in another application, use the Save As command which is accessible from the File menu. Outlook will ask you to give it a name and will then allow you to reopen and modify it in the application of your choice.

To save an item:

1. Click on the item in the folder (or create it).
2. Click on **File**, then select **Save As** (see Figure 11.1).

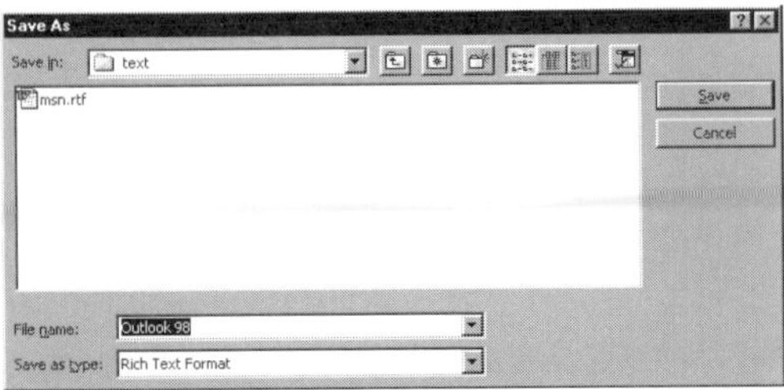

Figure 11.1: The Save As box allows you to choose the disk or the folder where you want to save your item

3. Select the drive and/or folder.
4. Enter the name of your item.
5. Select the file type (see Table 11.1).
6. Click on **Save**.

Table 11.1: Various file types available for saving.

File type	Description
Text Only	Saves in ASCII format. This file type can be opened in any text editor.
RTF	Saves in Rich Text Format. This file type can be opened in other applications such as Word, Lotus Notes, etc.

Table 11.1: Various file types available for saving (cont.).

File type	Description
Outlook Template	Saves your item as a template to act as a basis for the creation of other items.
Message Format	Saves in a format usable for e-mail messages.

If you want to save an item and the Save As command is not accessible, select the item before clicking on Save As.

Opening an item saved in another application

You have saved a task called News, for example, as an RTF file. You need this item in a Word document.

To open an item from another application:

1. Double-click on the Word shortcut icon in the Windows Desktop.
2. Click on **File**, then select **Open**.

   The Open box is displayed (see Figure 11.2).
3. Select the drive and/or the folder.
4. Select the type RTF.
5. Click on the file you want (in our example: News).
6. Click on **Open**.

Whatever the type of file to be opened, the procedure is the same in any application.

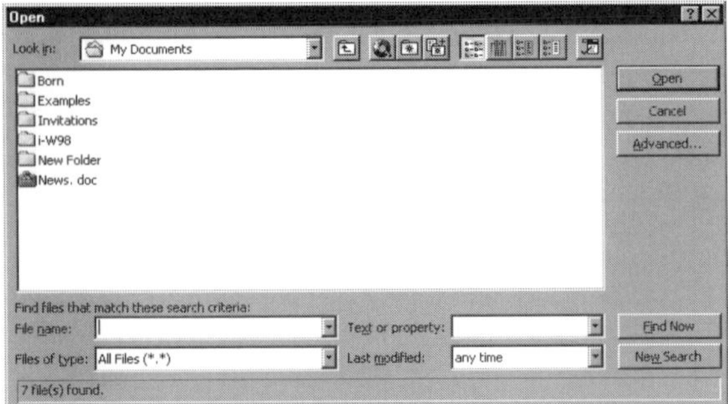

Figure 11.2: The Open dialog box allows you to find the document or file you want to open

FINDING ITEMS

If you receive and send many messages, or often assign and receive tasks, the Find function can be very useful.

You use the Find command, present in each toolbar, to access the find pane. This pane varies according to the type of item you are looking for, but its use is the same.

1. Click on **Find** in the toolbar of the folder you are in (see Figure 11.3).

Figure 11.3: The Find button

2. Enter the item you are looking for in the **Look for** field.
3. Click on **Find Now**.

   If the search is successful, the result will be displayed in the form of a table at the bottom of the Find box (see Figure 11.4).

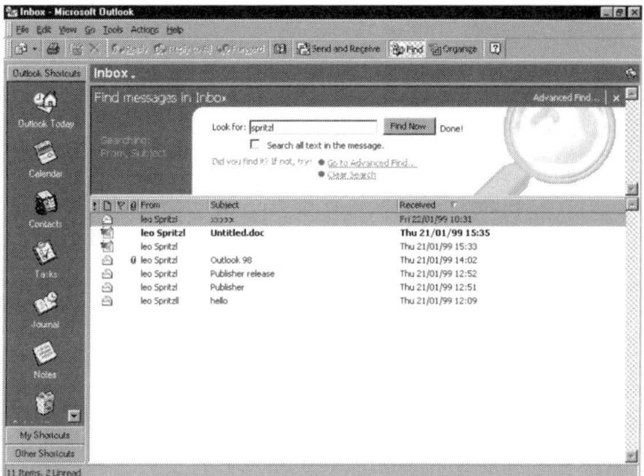

Figure 11.4: The result of the search is displayed at the bottom of the box

4. Double-click on the icon of the item to open it.

5. When you have finished consulting the item, click on **File**, then **Close**.

6. Click on the **Close** button in the Find pane or click on **Find** in the toolbar to deactivate it.

The pane of the Find command varies depending on the item you are looking for.

Find function options

When you run the find operation and it is unsuccessful, Outlook offers advanced find options. Click on **Advanced Find** in the find pane. Table 11.2 describes the options accessible in each of the first find tabs.

Table 11.2: The options in the Contacts tab of the Advanced Find box.

Option	Description
Search for the word(s)	To enter a detail such as the name, the company, the town, etc.
In	To select the desired search field (file, name, address, etc.)
E-mail (address)	To enter the URL of the contact
Time	To enter the creation date of the item
Find Now	To run the search when the different fields have been filled in
New Search	To perform a new search

Outlook offers these Find function tabs for a more refined search if you cannot find the item you are looking for.

More Choices tab

Using this tab, you can access other options to refine the item search. The options are as follows (see Figure 11.5):

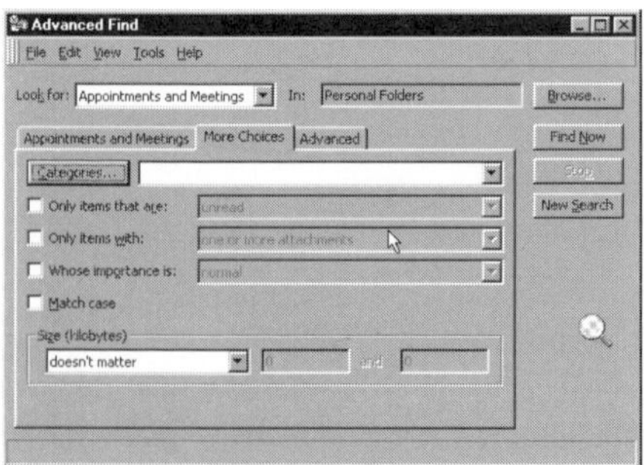

Figure 11.5: The More Choices tab in the Advanced Find box

- **Categories.** By clicking on this option, you can choose a category for the item sought. This option is accessible for all types sought.
- **Only items that are.** By ticking this option, you can find read or non-read items. This option is accessible for all types sought.
- **Only items with.** By ticking this option, you can find items with or without attachments.
- **Whose importance is.** By ticking this option, you can find items of normal, high or low importance. This option is accessible for finding messages, tasks, appointments or meetings.
- **Match case.** By ticking this option, you can search for an item whose file name is written in exactly the same case (upper and/ or lower case).
- **Size (kilobytes).** By clicking on the arrow, you open a list where you can choose to search through items of a certain size only.

To cancel the search criteria and enter others, simply click on ***New Search*** *and enter new criteria in the search fields.*

The Advanced tab

Using the **Advanced** tab, you can add search fields or criteria (see Figure 11.6).

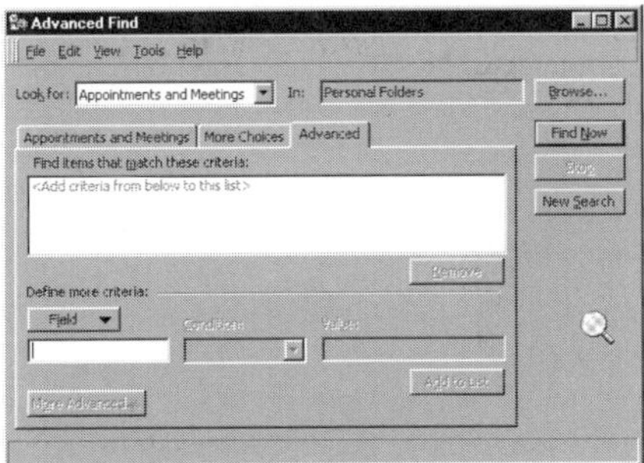

Figure 11.6: The Advanced tab of the Advanced Find box

1. Click on **Field**.
2. Select the field category you want (see Figure 11.7).

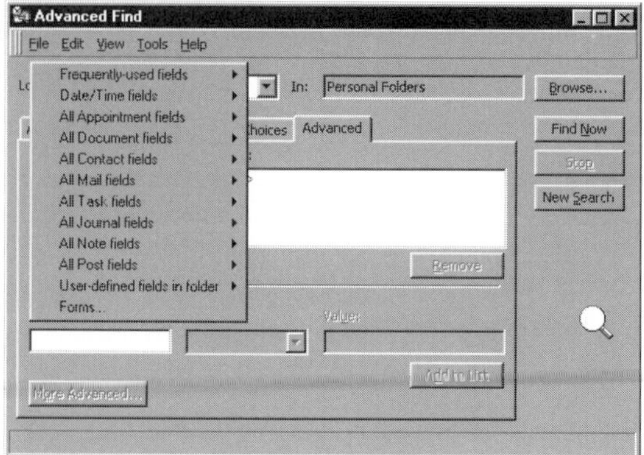

Figure 11.7: The Field button menu

3. Click on the field type.
4. The chosen field is displayed in the **Advanced** tab. Click on the arrow in the **Condition** option. Select the condition you want.
5. Enter the value of the search condition in the **Value** option.
6. Click on **Add to the List**.

   The search conditions you have just specified are displayed in the **Find items that match these criteria** field. You can, of course, specify other search criteria.
7. When you have finished indicating the search criteria, click on **Find Now**.

   The result will be displayed in a table at the bottom of the box.
8. Double-click on the icon opposite the search result to open the item found.

9. When you have finished, from within the item click on **File**, then select **Close**.
10. Click on the **Close** button in the Advanced Find dialog box.

Linking items

You can create different items such as a task, a contact or a note from another Outlook item. You can also insert an item into a task. Linking items cancels the need to print out a message or a note in order to be able to refer to it whilst you are working on another task; you need only insert it in the item to be able to refer to it at any time.

Linking Outlook items

Here you will learn how to create messages or appointments from an Outlook item.

Creating an appointment from a message

You have received a message from one of your customers inviting you to an appointment. As a reminder, you want to insert it in your Schedule.

1. In the Inbox, click on the message concerned, without opening it, then drag it to Calendar in the Outlook Shortcuts bar.

   The Appointment box is displayed. Some of the information contained in the message is shown in the Appointment box (see Figure 11.8).
2. Enter the location of the appointment.
3. Make any required changes.
4. Click on **Save and Close** in the toolbar when you have finished.

   Your new appointment is displayed in the Schedule.

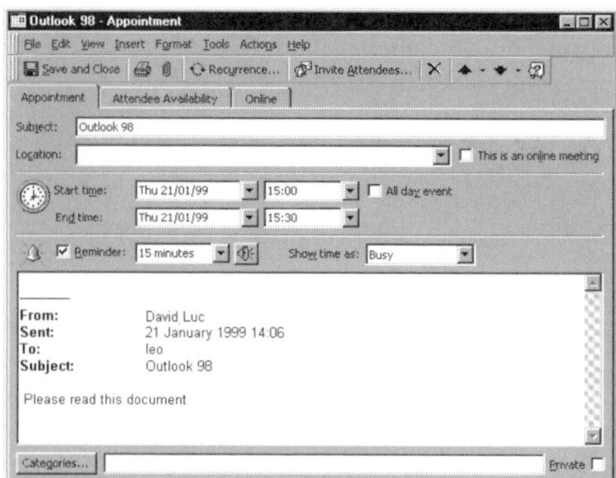

Figure 11.8: When you drag a message to the Calendar, the Appointment box is displayed

Creating a task from a message

A message sent to you requires the performance of a certain job. You must therefore create a task to remind you of the work to be carried out.

To create a task related to the message:

1. In the Inbox, click on the message concerned, without opening it, then drag it to **Tasks** in the Outlook Shortcuts bar.

   The Task box is displayed. Some of the information contained in the message is shown in the Task box (see Figure 11.9).

2. Make any changes required.
3. Enter the options applicable to the tasks (due date, importance, etc.).
4. Click on **Save and Close** in the toolbar when you have finished.

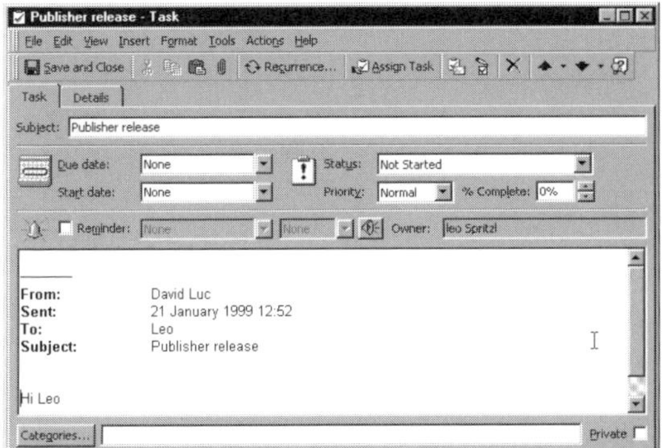

Figure 11.9: When you drag a message to the Tasks folder, the Task box opens

When you drag a message to another Outlook folder, it does not disappear from the Inbox. Outlook copies this message to the new folder and keeps the original in the Inbox.

Creating a note from an Outlook item

Whatever folder you are working in, Outlook allows you to create a note from an item. This is possible in all folders: Calendar, Tasks, Inbox and Journal.

To create a note from any item:

1. Click on the item for which you want to create a note, without opening it; you can do this in any folder.
2. Drag the item to **Notes** in the Outlook Shortcuts bar.

   Outlook automatically creates and displays the note (see Figure 11.10).
3. Make your changes.
4. Click on the **Close** button when you have finished.

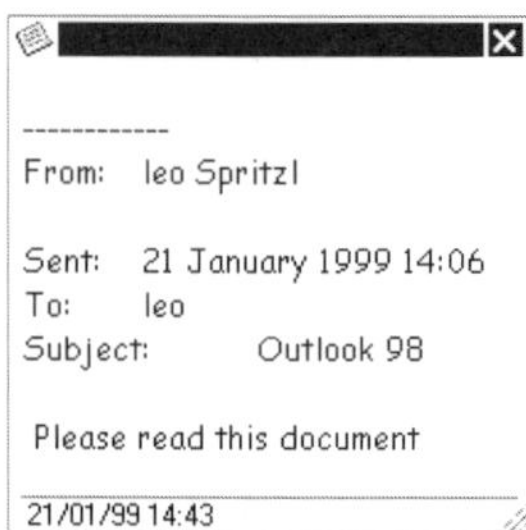

Figure 11.10: The note is automatically created and displays the content of the item from which it has been created

Linking with other Office applications

You can easily create a new document for an application (Word, Excel, etc.) from Outlook. For example, say you want to incorporate an Excel worksheet in the Tasks folder.

To create a new Office document in Outlook:

1. In the desired folder, click on **File**, then select **New** and drag to open the sub-menu.
2. Click on **Office Document**.

   The New Office Document box is displayed (see Figure 11.11).
3. Click on the document.
4. Click on **OK**.

   A dialog box is displayed, and you have the option of:

   – posting the document in the folder, which means it will be listed in the folder where you were when you chose your new document, or

   – sending the document to someone, which means that when you have finished creating your new document, the Message box will be displayed and you will be able to send this document to your addressee.

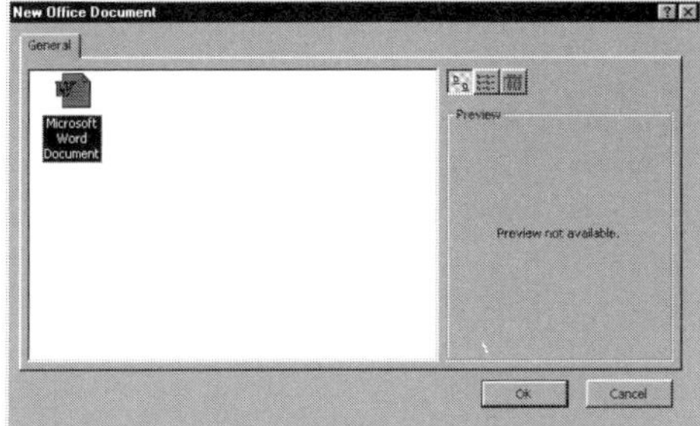

Figure 11.11: In the New Office Document box you choose the type of document you want to insert

5. Tick the box of the option you want, then click on **OK**.

   The new document is displayed in your folder (see Figure 11.12).

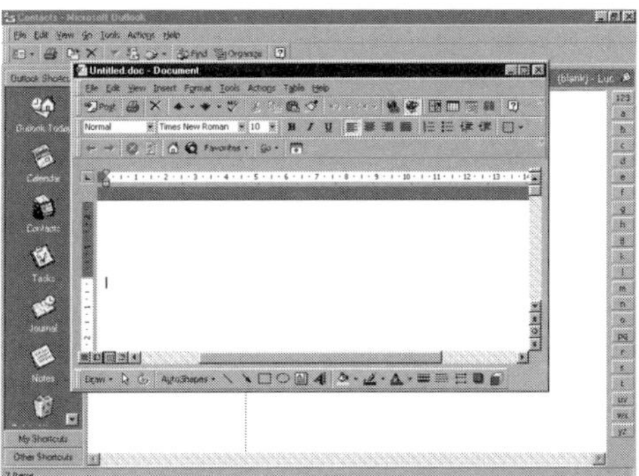

Figure 11.12: The new document is displayed in your folder

6. Enter your information and carry out any formatting.
7. Click on **Post** to send your document to the folder.
8. Click on **File**, then select **Close**.

The document you have just created will be displayed in the active folder.

Incorporating linked objects

Outlook allows you to incorporate files which will be inserted using an Office application and will be linked to it, i.e. all modifications made to the source file (Excel, Word, etc.) will also immediately be made to the inserted file. This concept is the OLE (Object Linking and Embedding) link which allows you to share data between Office applications. For example, imagine you have incorporated an Excel table in one of your contacts. This table is managed in Excel and concerns sales achieved with this contact. Each time you change a data item in the table using Excel, these modifications will automatically be made to the table inserted in Outlook. In the same way, if you modify this table in Outlook, these modifications will also be made to the relevant Excel file.

To incorporate a file, a table, etc., in an Outlook item:

1. In the folder concerned, create the new item or double-click on it to open it.
2. Place the pointer in the text field and click.
3. Click on **Insert**, then select **Object**.

   The Insert Object box is displayed (see Figure 11.13).

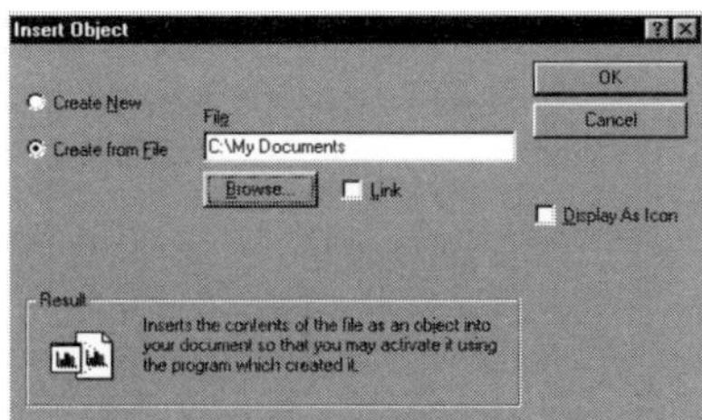

Figure 11.13: In the Insert Object box, you select the source file

4. Click on the **Create from File** option.
5. Click on the **Link** option.

6. Click on **Browse**.
7. Click on the arrow in the **Look In** field.
8. Click on the desired file in the list and click on **OK**.
9. In the Insert Object box, click on **OK**.

   The inserted file is displayed (see Figure 11.14).

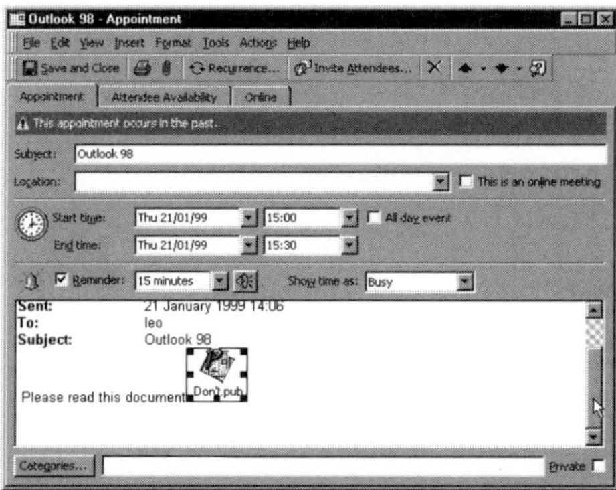

Figure 11.14: The inserted file is displayed in the text field

USING TEMPLATES

When you create messages, appointments and meetings, you can choose to use different types of items using various fonts, decorative items, etc.

To use an Outlook template:

1. In the folder corresponding to the item you want to create, click on **File**, then select **New**.
2. Drag to the right to open the drop-down menu and select **Choose Form**.

   The Form dialog box is displayed (see Figure 11.15).

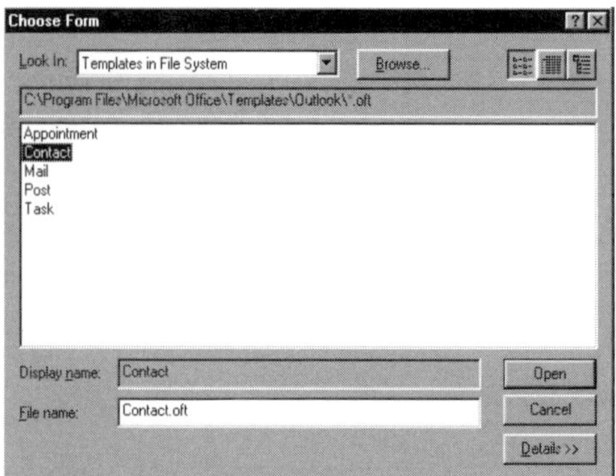

Figure 11.15: The Form box offers a number of templates for creating appointments, messages, etc.

3. Select the **Templates in File System** option in the **Look In** field.
4. Select the template you want, then click on **Open**.

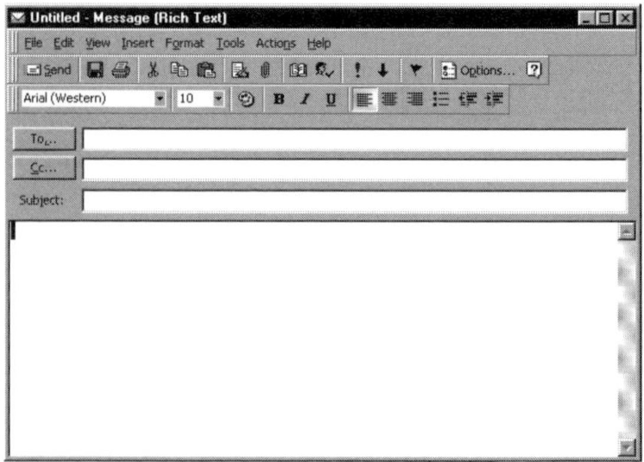

Figure 11.16: The Message box opens, displaying a formatting bar and a drawing bar

5. Enter your text and format it using these tools.
6. When you have finished, click on **Send** or on **Save and Close** according to the type of item created.

Table 11.3: Keyboard shortcuts for Hour 11.

Action	Keyboard shortcut
Open	**Ctrl-O**
Find items	**Ctrl-Shift-F**
New Office document	**Ctrl-Shift-H**

Hour 12

The Internet and Outlook

The contents for this hour

- Introduction to the Internet
- The Web
- Connection to the Internet
- Using the Internet in Outlook

Introduction to the Internet

The Internet consists of millions of interconnected computers which communicate, send each other messages and share information.

The Internet came into being in the United States during the 1970s, originally as Arpanet (Advanced Research Projects Agency network), which was the computer system of the US Defense Department, and subsequently spread into government networks. Today, the Internet is world-wide and links millions of computers.

The different services provided by the Internet

The Internet offers many types of services, including:

- **WWW *(World Wide Web).*** This is a hypertext system which allows you to display a document, then to make another document appear by clicking on a link within the original document, and so on. It offers text, sound, images and videos. In this Hour, the WWW will be referred to as the Web.
- **FTP *(File Transfer Protocol).*** Using FTP, you can transfer or download files to and from anywhere in the world.
- **Gopher.** This is a menu service which allows you to navigate from one computer to another to find documents.
- **IRC *(Internet Relay Chat).*** This service allows you to talk in real time with other people throughout the world.

This list is necessarily limited, since the Internet offers dozens of services, but it includes the main services.

Hypertext is a coloured, underlined word or group of words offering links to other documents or pages. Simply click on a hypertext link to display a new Web document.

THE WEB

The Web is the most widely used Internet service. It consists of millions of electronically linked documents. In the Web, you navigate from document to document or go directly to a document by indicating its URL address to your Web browser (Web navigation program).

The address or URL (Universal Resource Locator) is made up of a protocol (such as http*), the name of the domain or site and the path indicating the server, e.g.:* http://www.server/wordlnet.com.

Navigating on the Web

When you navigate on the Web using Outlook, you will first arrive at the home page of a site you have chosen. The home page is the main page of a Web site. You begin your navigation from it by clicking on a hypertext link or on an image. Hypertext links and images, which open another document, are usually underlined or in a different colour than the rest of the text, and are indicated by the appearance of a little hand on the screen when you move the mouse cursor on to them.

The toolbar of the browser which you open by activating the Web from Outlook allows you move around in the open pages or documents.

Here are a few buttons found on the toolbar of a browser:

- **Home.** Allows you to return to the home page.
- **Back.** Allows you to return to the previous page.
- **Forward.** Allows you to go to the next page.
- **Print.** Allows you to print the current Web page.

The browser has a bar of rapid access buttons from which you can very quickly view a Web site.

The buttons of a browser rapid access bar are as follows:

- **News.** Allows you to open a document containing information on new Web sites.
- **To See.** Allows you to open a document containing information on interesting Web sites.
- **Destinations.** Allows you to access the best Web sites by category.
- **Net Search.** Allows you to access Web search engines.
- **People.** Allows you to search by name, type, etc.

Similar buttons and toolbars for browsing the Web are also available in Netscape Navigator and Communicator.

Connection to the Internet

From Outlook, you can access the Web and use Internet e-mail. But first, you must be connected to the Internet.

There are two ways of connecting to the Internet:

- by modem; or
- via your company network.

Connecting by modem

To be able to use a connection, you must be a subscriber to an Internet Service Provider (ISP) who will give you the installation parameters for the connection, your password, your domain, your account name, your TCP/IP address, and so on.

An ISP is a company that provides you with access to the Internet via a server (host computer).

The connection procedures are as follows:

- installing a TCP/IP protocol;
- installing Dial-Up Networking; and
- creating a connection to the ISP.

Installing a TCP/IP protocol

To connect to the Internet, a TCP/IP protocol must be installed. This is a one-off procedure which is performed the first time the modem is used for the Internet connection; you will not have to do it again.

To install a TCP/IP protocol:

1. In the Windows Desktop, click on **Start** in the Taskbar.
2. Click on **Settings**, then select **Control Panel**.
3. Double-click on the **Network** icon.

   The Network box is displayed (see Figure 12.1).

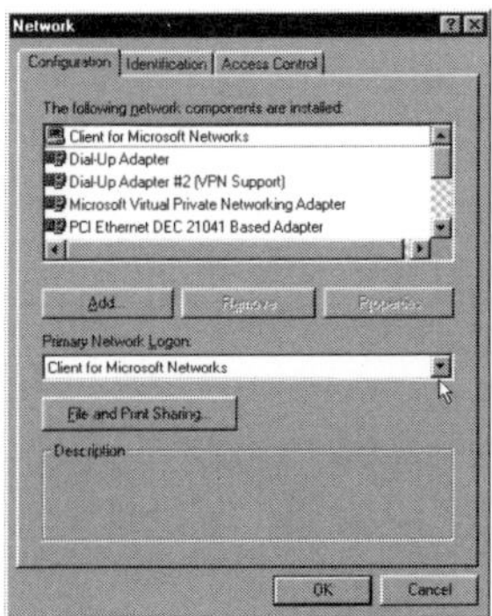

Figure 12.1: The Network box

4. Click on **Add**.
5. Click on the **Adapter** icon and click on **Add**.

   The Select Network adapters box is displayed (see Figure 12.2).

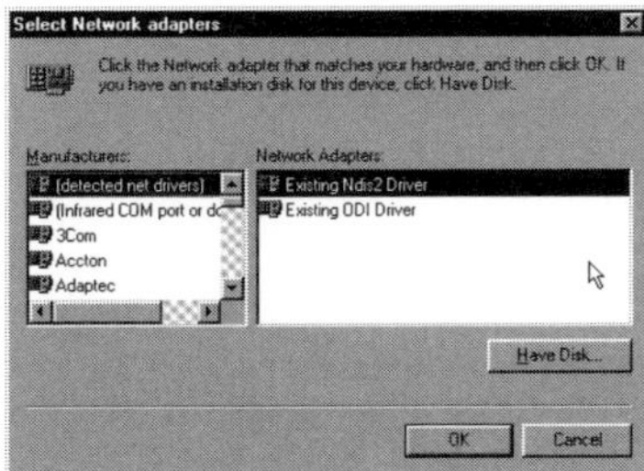

Figure 12.2: The Select Network adapters box

6. Click on [detected net drivers].
7. Click on **OK**.

   The Network box is displayed.
8. Click on **TCP/IP**, then on **Properties**.

   The TCP/IP Properties box is displayed.
9. Click on the **IP Address** tab.
10. Tick **Obtain an IP Address Automatically**.
11. Click on the **WINS Configuration** tab, then tick **Disable WINS Resolution**.
12. Click on the **Gateway** tab, then enter the number supplied by the ISP.
13. Click on the **DNS Configuration** tab, then tick **Enable DNS**.
14. In the **Host** field, enter the name of your ISP.
15. In the **Domain** field, enter the domain of the ISP.
16. In the **DNS Server Search Order** field, enter the primary DNS supplied by the ISP, then click on **Add**.
17. In the same field, enter the secondary DNS supplied by the ISP, then click on **Add**.
18. Click on **OK**.
19. Click on **OK** in the Network box.
20. Click on **Yes** in the **Modify System Parameters** box.

    You have now installed the TCP/IP protocol.

Installing Dial-Up Networking

You must now install Dial-Up Networking. This is also a one-off procedure which is performed the first time the modem is used for the Internet connection; you will not have to do it again.

Here is the procedure:

1. Click on **Start**, then select **Settings**.
2. Click on **Control Panel**.
3. Double-click on the **Add/Remove Programs** icon.
4. Click on the **Windows Setup** tab.
5. In the **Components** field, click on **Communications**.
6. Click on Details, then tick **Dial-Up Networking.**
7. Click on **OK** in the Communications box.
8. Click on **OK** in the Add/Remove Programs Properties box.
9. If necessary, insert the Windows 95 CD and follow the procedure.

   You have now installed Dial-Up Networking.

Creating a connection to the ISP

Now that you have installed the TCP/IP protocol and Dial-up Networking, you can install the ISP connection, which you will only subsequently have to double-click in order to access the Net.

To create the connection:

1. Click on **Start**, then select **Programs**.
2. Click on **Accessories** and select **Dial-Up Networking**.
3. Double-click on **Make New Connection**.

   The Make New Connection box is displayed (see Figure 12.3).
4. Click on **Next**.
5. Enter the name of the host server.
6. Click on **Next**.
7. Enter the telephone number.

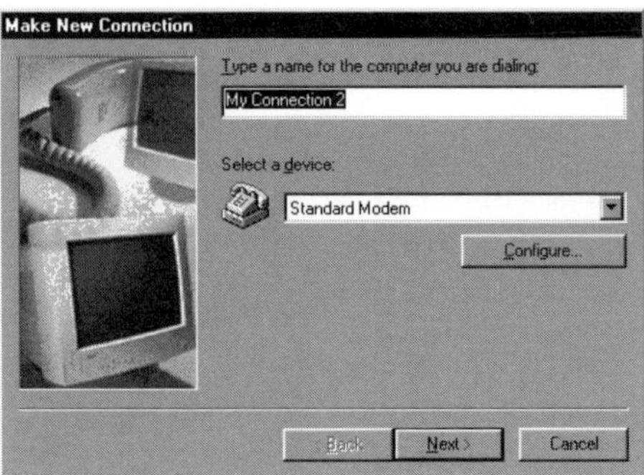

Figure 12.3: The Make New Connection box

8. Click on **Next**.
9. Click on **Finished**.

To initiate the connection:

1. Click on **Start**, then select **Programs**.
2. Click on **Accessories**.
3. Double-click on the host server connection icon.

   The Connect To box is displayed (see Figure 12.4)

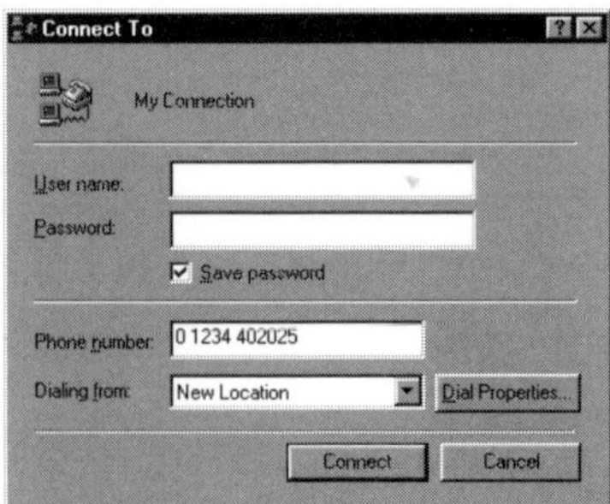

Figure 12.4: The Connect To box displaying your connection status

4. Click on **Connect**.

   The connection is initiated (see Figure 12.5).

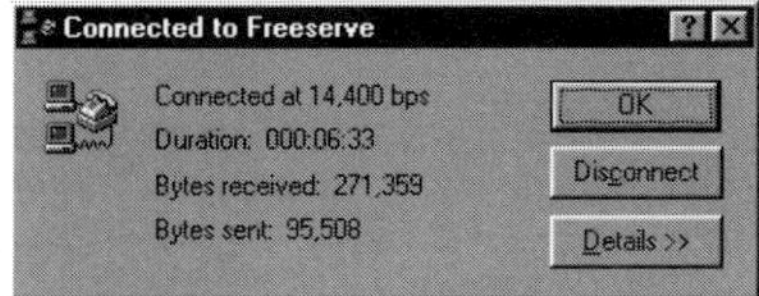

Figure 12.5: The Connected To (name of your ISP) box

Connecting via your company network

The connection is made by your company's network Administrator. You need only click on Internet from Outlook.

Using the Internet in Outlook

You can access two Internet services using Outlook:

- the Web; and
- Internet e-mail.

Browsing the Web using Outlook

Don't forget that to browse the Web you must have a browser (i.e. Netscape Navigator or Internet Explorer). In the figures shown in this Hour, the browser illustrated is Internet Explorer 4.0. This is the standard Microsoft browser and is currently the most widely used browser world-wide.

A browser is the program which allows you to navigate through the pages of the Web. As an analogy, imagine that the Internet is a television set and the browser is the remote control unit.

To access the Web:

1. In Outlook, click on **Help**, then select **Microsoft on the Web**.

   Outlook opens a drop-down menu (see Figure 12.6).

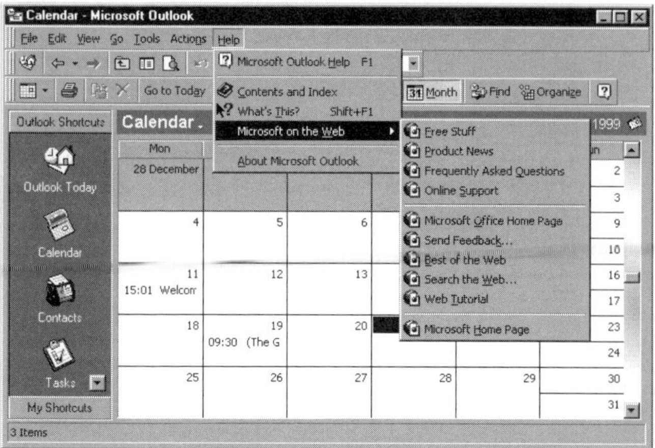

Figure 12.6: The Microsoft on the Web drop-down menu

2. Click on one of the drop-down menu commands.

   The browser is automatically launched.

   You arrive at the page chosen from the drop-down menu; you are now on the Web (see Figure 12.7).

3. If necessary, enter the URL address of the Web page you want to open.

4. When you have finished, click on **File,** then **Close** to close the browser.

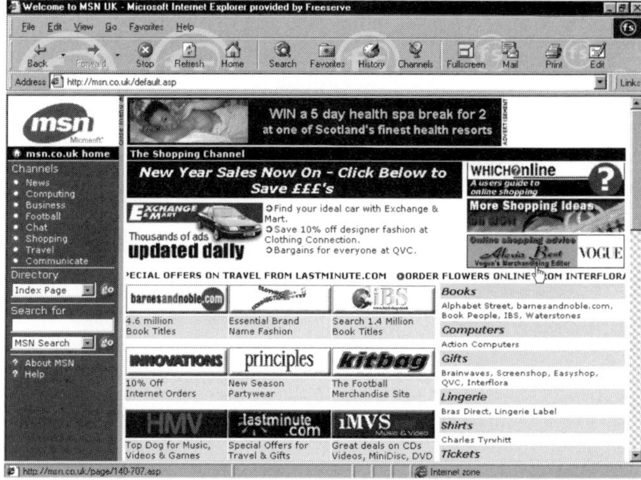

Figure 12.7: The home page of Microsoft Office on the Web

Table 12.1: The options offered in the drop-down menu of Microsoft on the Web.

Action	Description
Free Stuff	Allows you to access a site from which you can download Microsoft utility programs free of charge
Product News	Allows you to access a site from which you can consult additional information about Outlook
Frequently Asked Questions	Allows you to access a newsgroup about Outlook
Online support	Allows you to access the Outlook technical support Web page

Table 12.1: The options offered in the drop-down menu of Microsoft on the Web (cont.).

Action	Description
Microsoft Office Home Page	Allows you to access the Office 97 home page
Send Feedback	Allows you to access a Web page from which you can send comments to Microsoft
Best of the Web	Allows you to access a Web page from which you can open hypertext links to the best sites selected by Microsoft
Search the Web	Allows you to access a Web page from which you can access search engines
Web Tutorial	Allows you to access online help on Internet browsing
Microsoft Home Page	Allows you to access the home page of the Microsoft company

Each time you open one of the commands of the Microsoft on the Web drop-down menu, you open your browser.

The Web in Contacts

Some of your customers, suppliers, friends, etc., may have pages on the Internet. To access their Web page you must enter their URL in their Contacts record.

To insert a Web address in a contact record:

1. Click on **Contacts** in the Outlook Bar.

2. Click on **New Contact** in the toolbar or double-click on the Address Card of the contact in which you want to indicate the address of the Web page.

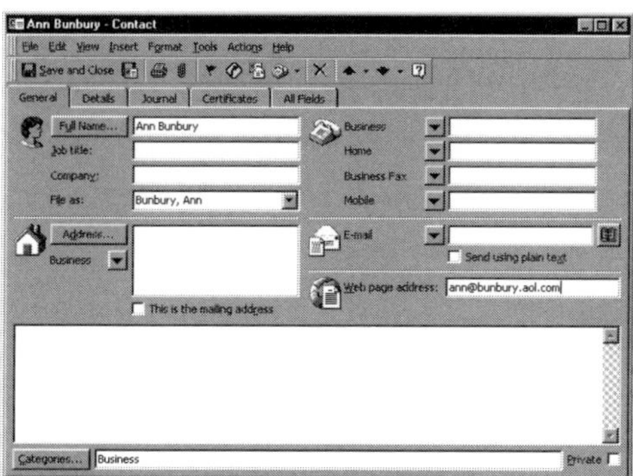

Figure 12.8: The Contacts record

3. Enter the URL in the Web page address field.
4. Enter the e-mail address of your contact in the E-mail field.
5. Click on **Save and Close**.

Now you have entered the various URLs of your contacts, you can open their Web pages from Outlook. Remember that you must be connected to the Internet to access a Web page.

To access the Web page of a contact:

1. In the Contacts folder, double-click on the **Address Card** of your contact.
2. Click on the URL of the contact.

   The browser is launched and you arrive at the Web page of your contact.

For more information on navigation on the Web, see a book specifically on Netscape Communicator or Internet Explorer.

Index

A

B

C

D

E

F

G

H

I

N